The Recruiting Officer

GEORGE FARQUHAR

The Recruiting Officer

THE NATIONAL THEATRE PRODUCTION

EDITED BY

Kenneth Tynan

RUPERT HART-DAVIS
Soho Square London W1
1965

All photographs in this volume
appear by kind permission of
Lewis Morley

Printed and bound in England by
Hazell Watson & Viney Ltd Aylesbury Bucks

Contents

Introduction

To put it crisply, what this book contains is all you need (and almost all there is) to know about the National Theatre's highly successful production of Farquhar's *The Recruiting Officer*, which opened at the Old Vic on 10 December 1963. It was the fourth production in the company's short history, which had begun on October 22 with *Hamlet* (directed by Laurence Olivier: Peter O'Toole as the prince), followed by Shaw's *Saint Joan* and Chekhov's *Uncle Vanya*. *Hamlet* was a *mise en scène d'occasion* and a play in which both director and star had appeared before. The Shaw and the Chekhov were transfers from the Chichester Festival. All three were acclaimed, especially *Vanya*; but *The Recruiting Officer* was the first National Theatre production to which everyone involved came absolutely fresh, and that is why we have chosen it as the subject of our first publication.

This is not primarily meant to be a souvenir volume. Rather, it is a blue-print; a permanent record of a theatrical event in all its aspects; a detailed, illustrated account of a production that did for an English classic the kind of service a National Theatre exists to provide—that of cleaning away the accretions of dust and over-painting with which time has disfigured the text, and bringing out the colours and forms of the original in all their pristine vivacity. In other words, this book is a sort of guided tour; and if it proves helpful to theatre workers, students of drama or anyone who wants to know how a particular group of actors tackled the problems of a particular play, it will have served its purpose. We hope to follow it up with similar studies of other N.T. productions.

Kenneth Tynan

Historical note

> WORTHY   And pray, what induced you to turn soldier?
>
> SERJEANT KITE   Hunger and ambition.
> *The Recruiting Officer*, Act III, Scene 1

The Recruiting Officer is a comedy whose invisible protagonist is war—to be precise, the War of the Spanish Succession, which broke out in 1702, four years before the play was performed. Fear of the ambitious French had been endemic in England for several decades; and when Louis XIV succeeded in putting his grandson on the Spanish throne—thereby achieving French control of the Western Mediterranean and of Spain's American Empire—he was challenged by a hostile coalition consisting of England, Holland, Denmark, Germany, Austria, Portugal and Savoy. At Blenheim in 1704 the great military partnership of Marlborough and Prince Eugene of Savoy won the first of a series of resounding victories. By the Treaty of Utrecht, which ended the war in 1713, the French nominee remained king in Madrid; but Spain was forced to make vast territorial concessions to the Grand Alliance; and France herself was exhausted.

George Farquhar spent much of his short life in close proximity to war. He was born in Ireland in 1677, and his birthplace, Derry, became the stronghold of the Northern Protestants in their revolt against James II. His father was a clergyman whose rectory was burned down by James' army in 1689. It has been testified (though never proved) that when William III landed in Ireland in 1690, the 13-year-old Farquhar volunteered for service in his army and took part in the Battle of the Boyne.

He was educated at Trinity College, Dublin, and briefly acted at the Smock Alley Theatre. Here he met the great comedian Robert Wilks, for whom he later wrote many leading parts—notably Sir Harry Wildair in *The Constant Couple*, Captain Plume in *The Recruiting Officer* and Archer in *The Beaux' Stratagem*. With Wilks' help he went to London and wrote his first play, *Love and a Bottle*, produced at Drury Lane in 1698. Its hero—a self-portrait—was George Roebuck, 'an Irish gentleman, of a wild roving temper, newly come to London'. A year later, at the age of 22, he made his reputation with *The Constant Couple*, as volatile a comedy as any of its time.

Bad days followed. His debts mounted, his plays failed, and he married a penniless woman in the belief that she was an heiress. In 1704, when his need for money was desperate, the Lord Lieutenant of Ireland commissioned him a lieutenant of Grenadiers; the pay—£54 15s. 0d. a year—helped towards keeping his family and pleasing his mistresses. He expected to be ordered to march with Marlborough to the Danube; instead, he was sent on recruiting duty to Lichfield and Shrewsbury.

The Mutiny and Impressment Acts of 1703–5 empowered Justices of the Peace 'to raise and levy such able-bodied men as have not any lawful calling or employment, or visible means for their maintenance and livelihood, to serve as soldiers.' The openings for corruption were many. As a recruiting officer, you could get a man drunk, slip some of the Queen's money into his pocket, and claim that he was thereby 'listed'.

Out of his Shrewsbury sojourn Farquhar fashioned an autobiographical play—the only Restoration comedy of note whose whole action is set in the country, among local gentry and countrymen, away from the nobility and

8

Other Recruits, Other Wars

the coffee-houses of London. 'Written in obvious high spirits within a few weeks in the early winter of 1705-6,' says Farquhar's biographer Willard Connely, '*The Recruiting Officer* expressed a joy of life not seen in Farquhar's work since his earliest effort.'— All the principal characters were based on people he had met, most of them residents of Shrewsbury. Silvia, for instance, the forthright, resolute, 'natural' woman—a new figure in the gallery of Restoration heroines—was Miss Laconia Berkeley, daughter of the local Deputy Recorder.

Farquhar submitted the play for approval to his superior officers: 'My recruits,' he said, 'were reviewed by my General and my Colonel, and could not fail to pass muster.' He took the script to London, where it was staged at Drury Lane in April 1706, with clamorous success. Wilks played Plume to Colley Cibber's Brazen; and Silvia was Farquhar's beloved Anne Oldfield, whom he had discovered working as a barmaid eight years before—'this jewel I found by accident in a tavern.' The play was constantly revived throughout the eighteenth century. Peg Woffington was a famous Silvia; as an amateur, aged 11, Garrick played Kite, and later (1741–2) appeared as the rustic Pearmain and Captain Plume. The last London production was staged at the Arts Theatre in 1943, with Trevor Howard in the lead.

Farquhar wrote one more play, *The Beaux' Stratagem*, presented in 1707. In April of the same year, aged 29, he died of TB in a garret overlooking St Martin's Lane.

Sir John Falstaff, in the first part of Shakespeare's *Henry IV*, meditates on the men he has pressed into service:
'If I be not ashamed of my soldiers, I am a soused gurnet. I have misused the king's press damnably. I have got, in exchange of a hundred and fifty soldiers, three hundred and odd pounds. I press me none but good householders, yeomen's sons; inquire me out contracted bachelors, such as had been asked twice on the banns; such a commodity of warm slaves, as had as lieve hear the devil as a drum; such as fear the report of a caliver worse than a struck fowl or a hurt wild-duck. I pressed me none but such toasts-and-butters, with hearts in their bellies no bigger than pins'-heads, and they have bought out their services; and now my whole charge consists of ancients, corporals, lieutenants, gentlemen of companies, slaves as ragged as Lazarus in the painted cloth, where the glutton's dogs licked his sores; and such as indeed were never soldiers, but discarded unjust serving-men, younger sons to younger brothers, revolted tapsters, and ostlers trade-fallen; the cankers of a calm world and a long peace, ten times more dishonourable than an old-faced ancient; and such have I, to fill up the rooms of them that have bought out their services, that you would think that I had a hundred and fifty tatter'd prodigals lately come from swine-keeping, from eating draff and husks. A mad fellow met me on the way and told me I had unloaded all the gibbets and pressed the dead bodies. . . .'

In *The Recruiting Sergeant*, a sharp-edged ballad-opera by Isaac Bickerstaff (1735–1812), the mother of a would-be soldier sings to the sergeant:

'Out upon thee, wicked locust!
  Worse in country nor a plague!
Men by thee are hocus-pocust
  Into danger and fatigue.
And the justices outbear thee
In thy tricks, but I don't fear thee,
  No, nor those that with thee league.
My son has enough at home.
He needs not for bread to roam:
Already his pay
Is twelvepence a day,
  His honest labour's fruits;
Then get thee a-trudging quick,
For 'gad! if I take a stick,
I'll make thee repent
When here thee were sent
  A-drumming for recruits.'

The Sergeant responds:

'What a charming thing's a battle!
Trumpets sounding, drums a-beating;
Crack, crick, crack, the cannons rattle;
Every heart with joy elating.
With what pleasure are we spying,
From the front and from the rear,
Round us in the smoky air,
  Heads and limbs and bullets flying!
  Then the groans of soldiers dying,
Just like sparrows, as it were.
  At each pop,
  Hundreds drop,
While the muskets prittle-prattle;
  Kill'd and wounded
  Lie confounded—
What a charming thing's a battle . . .
Kill's the word, both men and cattle;
  Then to plunder,
  Blood and thunder,
What a charming thing's a battle!'

Mother:
'Call you this charming? 'Tis the work of hell.'

Serjeant Musgrave's Dance (1959) by John Arden is set in a Northern town around 1880. Musgrave arrives with a recruiting party, bent on a fanatical mission—to avenge violence with violence. Annie, a barmaid, is asked 'what soldiers is good for':
'I'll tell you for what a soldier's good:
  To march behind his roaring drum,
  Shout to us all: "Here I come
  I've killed as many as I could—
  I'm stamping into your fat town
  From the war and to the war
  And every girl can be my whore
  Just watch me lay them squealing down."
  And that's what he does and so do we.
  Because we know he'll soon be dead
  We strap our arms round the scarlet red
  Then send him weeping over the sea. . . .
What good's a bloody soldier 'cept to be dropped into a slit in the ground like a letter in a box?'

Production Preface

WILLIAM GASKILL

Many people have asked me why I did not choose to direct Brecht's version of *The Recruiting Officer*. My answer was that if the original play had been by Schiller and not by Farquhar I might have, but that I saw no reason to put on an English translation of a German adaptation of a perfectly good English play. It is more pertinent to ask why Brecht should have chosen to adapt a comparatively little-known English classic.

No classic is timeless; at one period of history it may assume a particular relevance for its audience undreamt of by the author. For the 30's *Richard II* was another *Vortex*, when the audience saw its self-pitying hero as one of them, and for us today, Falstaff's questioning of honour in *Henry IV* is the same as Joan Littlewood's in *Oh, What a Lovely War!* The form and pressure of our time is essentially anti-heroic and we respond most to those writers like Middleton and Farquhar whose view of heroism is as sceptical as our own.

The Recruiting Officer is based on Farquhar's first-hand experience while recruiting in Shrewsbury. Within the conventional framework of Restoration comedy he set down his own detailed observation of the effect of a recruiting campaign on a small country town. He saw that the Act of Impressment, which gave the final say in forcible conscription to the Justices, was a mockery because they were in league with the army. He saw the ruthlessness of the officers who were sent to beat-up for Marlborough's army. He saw all this accurately but he was not indignant (he was one of the officers). Brecht took Farquhar's observation as the basis of his own indignation at the exploitation of the working class. He substantially rewrote the play in his own terms and set it in the War of American Independence. It would be false to impose on Farquhar Brecht's statement of the social situation but we cannot ignore in Farquhar those elements which excited Brecht to make his version.

There are no longer recruiting campaigns (except for Civil Defence), conscription has been abolished, and war is now in the hands of scientists and politicians. What is the particular compulsion for us, today, of the image of a group of soldiers arriving in a country town—the same image that John Arden used in *Serjeant Musgrave's Dance*? I think what we recognise from our experience is the systematic deception of the ignorant to a pointless end by the use of the heroic images of the past, a past no longer relevant. We may laugh at Pearmain and Appletree but we recognise our own plight.

We also have, in Plume and Silvia, a hero and heroine whose attitude to sex is as sensible and practical as we would like to imagine our own. When Plume says: 'Suppose I married a woman who wanted a leg—such a thing might be unless I examined the goods beforehand,' and Silvia says: 'Constancy is but a dull sleepy quality at best,' they are speaking way ahead of their time. Farquhar's genuine desire to find a solution for marital problems, so unlike the complacent acceptance of adultery of other Restoration writers, was the beginning of that social awareness in the works of Gay and Fielding which provoked Walpole to saddle us with the Lord Chamberlain and muzzled English drama for 200 years, until another Irishman, Bernard Shaw, took up where Farquhar left off.

11

Rehearsal Logbook

KENNETH TYNAN

In directing a play which observes social values without criticising them I have tried to make clear (without underlining) those points which will be more meaningful to a modern audience. To do more would be to destroy the framework in which Farquhar wrote, and would involve rewriting the play.

The Recruiting Officer was rehearsed for five weeks and some odd days. Its director, William Gaskill, came to the National Theatre on the strength of a high reputation gained at the Royal Court Theatre and at Stratford-upon-Avon. John Osborne's *Epitaph for George Dillon* (which he also staged on Broadway), and two plays by N. F. Simpson— *A Resounding Tinkle* and *One-Way Pendulum* —were among his Royal Court productions. For the Royal Shakespeare Company he directed *Richard III*, *Cymbeline*, Brecht's *Caucasian Chalk Circle* and *Infanticide in the House of Fred Ginger*, a stark and disturbing first play by Fred Watson. His last West End production before joining the N.T. as one of Olivier's two Associate Directors (the other being John Dexter) was Brecht's picaresque early work *Baal*, with Peter O'Toole in the leading role. Gaskill was born in Yorkshire, and when *The Recruiting Officer* opened he was thirty-three years old.

The notes that follow were jotted down during rehearsals. The N.T.'s temporary offices consist of a row of flimsy huts on a bomb-site near Waterloo Bridge, of which the Rehearsal Room is the largest. The Spartan surroundings, the frequent emergencies, the regular briefing sessions are all redolent of Biggin Hill. One has a distinct sense of participating in the theatrical equivalent of the Battle of Britain.

Week One

A striking beginning: Gaskill dispenses with the traditional read-through, explaining to the cast that the lines are the last stage of a process that must begin with a thorough investigation of character and situation. The first morning is devoted to improvisations unconnected with the text. Seated in a circle, the cast are told to pass an imaginary object from one to another; as each person receives the 'object' he must transform it by means of mime into something else. Next, Gaskill places a chair in the middle of the circle and challenges the actors to use it as something other than a chair. One rides it like a horse; another makes love to it; a third combs his hair with it. Then comes an exercise in association: Gaskill walks round the group carrying a brief-case, asking each actor to state spontaneously what it reminds him of. Finally, we have improvisation in pairs. Two people carry out an unrehearsed mime of their own choice (e.g. painting a wall). After watching them for a few moments, a third intervenes and changes the action into something else (e.g. a game of tennis). These exercises are a kind of limbering-up, psychological as well as physical. The aim, in Gaskill's words, is 'to help you relate to each other's imaginations.' He announces that every day before rehearsals he will hold an optional movement class, lasting half an hour.

Using a model of the set, Gaskill tells the cast where the scenery will be, but makes no attempt to dictate to them where they should move. He approaches each scene in four stages. (1) Seated, the actors read the text. (2) On their feet, and without scripts, they improvise on the basis of what they know of the scene: e.g., in I.1., Sergeant Kite's basic 'action' is to persuade the local lads to enlist, and theirs is to resist his efforts. (Gaskill makes great use of the terms 'action' and 'resistance'.) This scriptless exercise is repeated several times, with widely differing results. (3) Gaskill quizzes the actors about the social background and motivation of the characters they are playing: 'What do you do for a living? How much do you earn? Less or more than you would in the army? Would your wife mind if you enlisted?' etc. (4) They perform the scene again, this time with scripts. In all this, there is no directorial coercion: characterisation emerges by question and answer, trial and error. Among the more extrovert actors I note a tendency—probably unavoidable—to go for glib laughs during the improvisations by merely replacing period idiom with modern slang.

Gaskill to cast: 'I know you're all skilled comic performers—otherwise you wouldn't be here. I take that skill for granted. But what audiences live on is the *relationships* between characters. And that means going to the sub-text—the real action that underlies the words spoken.' He cares little at this stage for externals, and never suggests business.

Max Adrian's baptism of improvisation: not, I should say, this fine actor's natural mode, though he tackles it bravely. Someone asks Gaskill the point of improvisation. He replies: 'To establish a sequence of emotions in the actor's mind.' Directing Adrian, he bids him remember that Justice Balance's surface bonhomie is not fundamental to his character; his class interests as a J.P. and a landowner are what really govern his behaviour. These must be revealed if the part is to be honestly played. Similarly, Gaskill says of I.1.: 'Recruiting isn't *fun* to Kite and Plume, although the scene itself is comic. It's their living and they're ruthless about it. You've got to show that. Otherwise the laughs are superficial.'

Olivier, absent for the first few days of rehearsal because of administrative duties, joins the group. He and Gaskill have not worked together before: one wonders whether they will see eye to eye (which in theatre means ego to ego). Once having seized on the emotional core of a part, Olivier usually pays fanatically fastidious attention to details of movement, business, costume, make-up, vocal inflexion, etc.; Gaskill, by contrast, stresses motives, 'drives', 'pressures', etc., seldom mentioning externals. I expect tension when Olivier is asked to improvise. Forebodings unjustified: he plunges in with zest and great inventiveness. He improvises in character, but sometimes goes far beyond what actually takes place in the scene—i.e. he invents things for Brazen to do and say which are perfectly consistent with the character but which, when followed through, bring the scene to a different conclusion from Farquhar's. Thus by improvisation one can discover aspects of character overlooked or (for dramatic reasons) suppressed by the author!

At first Olivier's conception of Brazen is too foppish and perky—a sort of Mr Puff in uniform. Guiding him towards the right tone of boorishness and sleazy vulgarity, Gaskill points out that the world of *The Recruiting Officer* is quite different fron Congreve's: small-town realism is the keynote, with no urban airs and graces. Olivier responds and his lines begin to take on the elephantine loquacity of the pub bore.

General note from Gaskill on pronunciation: avoid coy archaisms such as 'obleege' for 'oblige' and 'avarsion' for 'aversion'.

Week Two

Maggie Smith hasn't yet found the right note of candour and directness for Silvia; she is tending to make her too sly. In the male impersonation scenes Robert Stephens (Plume) is having trouble addressing her as if he really accepts her as a man: he can't help being ever so slightly deferential and gallant. This is no fault of Maggie S.'s: the problem arises wherever breeches parts are concerned.

Dealing with the Court scene (V.5), Gaskill asks the cast to bear in mind the 'social subtext': Farquhar is demonstrating how Justice worked in cahoots with the Army to get recruits, in spite of the Act of Parliament forbidding such collusion. For example, Balance invites Plume to sit beside him on the bench, and Kite is allowed to describe himself as 'counsel for the Queen'. Of the three J.P.'s, Scruple alone takes any trouble to give the defendants a fair hearing. 'Balance,' says Gaskill, 'is really an old fascist.' The stage direction 'Plume reads the Articles of War' is to be literally interpreted: Gaskill has prepared a potted version of the Articles of War for 1706, to illustrate the immense variety of

offences for which the penalty was death.

His insistence on realism is already paying off. The actors are not falling back on the fussy extravagances that commonly pass for 'Restoration style'. He repeatedly warns the cast to cut gestures down to a minimum: the prose rhythms encourage manual flourishes, which must be resisted. The countrymen especially are to remember that after a day's work in the fields one's arms are tired and hang heavily.

II.3 (which ends with Plume's successful bid to trick Pearmain and Appletree into the army) is clearly going to be outstanding. It's very funny, yet the underlying ruthlessness comes powerfully across, and there's a bitter inevitability about Pearmain's final capitulation. Gaskill to Kite and the two victims: 'At the beginning of the scene, don't just play drunkenness—it's too easy. Don't obscure the social points the lines are making, like Appletree's remark that a J.P. is more powerful than any emperor.'

The longest scene in the play, IV.3, in which Kite dresses up as a German clairvoyant to ensnare recruits, hasn't yet got off the ground. It was obviously written as a set-piece for a virtuoso clown. Gaskill has added some effective bits of business (e.g. Kite spearing cards on his sword while telling Pluck's fortune) but now seems determined to cut them. His unwillingness to 'improve on' the text here works against him; I suspect that the scene was composed with just such 'improvements' in mind. (As finally acted, it was much reduced in length.)

By the end of the week, technical considerations—moves, sightlines, etc.—are starting to intrude: 'If I cross here, he can get round behind me without masking her . . .' But still no run-through.

Week Three

Maggie S. is settling into the breeches scenes with a deeper voice and a more convinced swagger; she now has the right air of dapper caddishness.

Improvisations are held on what has been

happening immediately before the play begins. Gaskill asks questions about the life of agricultural labourers in the early 17th century. How many hours a day did they work? Have they just come in from the fields when Kite arrives? Have they ever seen a recruiting officer before? (Answer: yes, it was probably an annual visitation; Plume's illegitimate child was sired during his last trip.) How much did they know about the laws relating to impressment? Do they approve of recruiting drives? (One member of the crowd says yes: it's better to send unemployed men overseas than keep them idle at the expense of the parish.) Were army conditions so much worse than their everyday lives? Gaskill adds: 'If you haven't any lines in this scene with Kite, you must find reasons for saying nothing.' From the improvisations the final form of the scene emerges. The townsfolk listen to Kite's sales-talk with no reaction at all: their 'resistance' expresses itself in sullen immobility, and Kite has to force them to pay attention.

The fortune-telling scene: Colin Blakely (Kite) is now giving a wonderfully subtle comic display, but on a scale rather too intimate for the Old Vic. Gaskill tells him: 'As an actor you tend to lose yourself in other people.'

Maggie S. discovers a very moving moment in her enlistment scene with Plume (IV.1). Her voice quavers just perceptibly when she says that no matter what perils life in the army may hold, 'they would be less terrible to me than to stay behind you'—and a twinge of genuine feeling disturbs the facade of badinage and imposture.

Week Four

The first full run-through: mood of general exhilaration. The recruiting scenes have been firmly earthed and the production will stand or fall by them. The Melinda–Worthy sub-plot is flimsier stuff, hard though the actors try to give it substance; and there isn't the right temperamental contrast (sincerity versus affectation) between Maggie S.'s Silvia and Mary Miller's Melinda. Some of the early expository passages with Balance, Pume and Silvia look static and too baldly 'plotty'. But no one's in any doubt that the basic structure is sound. Incidental music is to be confined to 'The British Grenadiers' and 'Over the Hills and Far Away', played on flute and fiddle; and it will be enough. Gaskill detests music when used as an adventitious, 'atmospheric' device.

The director's comments on the run-through: (1) some of the scenes that have been intensively rehearsed have become too casual and intimate—'the plot and action are getting lost between your noses'; (2) too many of the actors have acquired a habit of *launching* themselves into big speeches with a grunt, an exclamation or a slight stamp of the foot—'if you're properly prepared for the speech it should fly like an arrow from a bow. The flow should be as effortless as Mozart'; (3) there's still a tendency, at times, not to trust the text—to overstress, underline and wink at the audience: 'Only when it's been *proved* that a line doesn't work can you afford to regard it as less than pure gold.'

As an experiment, Gaskill makes Silvia and Melinda exchange roles in some of their scenes together—so that each can judge the other's character from the outside: the acting equivalent of seeing ourselves as others see us.

Throughout the week the final scene of discovery and reconciliation remains somewhat lifeless. My deadpan suggestion that the recruits should march in at the end with banners reading 'Marlborough Needs You' and 'Malplaquet By Christmas' is thanklessly spurned. The assistant director unearths a few curious phrases of military exhortation from an old army handbook: given to Brazen and delivered to the troops, they help to lift the closing moments.

First run-through on the Old Vic stage. Decision is taken to cut the Plume—Brazen exchange in V.4 where Brazen asks Plume's advice as to whether he should invest in a privateer or a playhouse. Olivier feels that, since he is investing his career in a national playhouse, it might sound too much like a private joke; and the lines aren't funny enough to justify the risk.

Week Five

Trouble with the court scene, which doesn't quite live up to the expectations aroused by its position in the play. The blame here is Farquhar's, for failing to clarify his heroine's motives. When the constable arrests the disguised Silvia on a charge of having raped the hoyden Rose, why is she so anxious to appear in court before Balance, her father? Answer, supplied by Gaskill: in Act II Balance has made Silvia promise never to marry without his consent. Hence her decision to dress as a man and enlist with her beloved Plume. But her sense of honour demands that her father should publicly and legally order her to go off with him. Hence her eagerness to be haled into court. But little of this is explicit in Farquhar's text; and short of rewriting, there is no way to make it so.

Gaskill enumerates the three principal 'actions' (or objectives) of the play, to which all else is ancillary:

(1) Silvia's determination to get Plume.

(2) Plume's and Kite's determination to get recruits.

(3) Worthy's determination to get Melinda.

Silvia's male impersonation brings (1) and (2) together; while Brazen's designs on Melinda link the recruiting theme with (3). Gaskill warns the cast that it is easy to lose sight of these vital objectives in the diffuse second half of the play—with resultant confusion in the audience's mind. From Silvia's point of view, he adds, the climax comes when she learns (in V.7) that Plume has agreed to discharge her from the army: this means that she has failed in her attempt to use the recruiting drive for her own romantic ends.

Gaskill decides to transpose V.5 and V.6: thus the Brazen–Worthy–Melinda sub-plot is settled before the court scene, which leads naturally into the Plume–Silvia dénouement.

Week Six

Dress rehearsals on Sunday and Monday. Gaskill watches each act from a different part of the house, checking sight-lines and audibility. Olivier broods over whether to use, as Brazen, the business of clicking his heels and getting the spurs entangled which he invented as Saranoff in *Arms and the Man*: he finally decides against it. The whirligig set works smoothly, and the cast is confident. Am I right in suspecting that, here and there, the text is not quite strong enough to stand up to the realistic scrutiny to which Gaskill has subjected it? Possibly. But this is a quibble, effectively silenced by the production as a whole. The play's muscles and bones have been trusted, tested and found to work. A Restoration masterpiece has been reclaimed, stripped of the veneer of camp that custom prescribes for plays of its period, and saved for the second half of the twentieth century.

Tuesday at 7: curtain up.

The Recruiting Officer

Mr Balance ⎫	Max Adrian
Mr Scale ⎬ three justices	Peter Cellier
Mr Scruple ⎭	Michael Turner
Mr Worthy, a gentleman of Shropshire	Derek Jacobi
Captain Plume ⎫ two recruiting officers	Robert Stephens
Captain Brazen ⎭	Laurence Olivier
Kite, sergeant to Plume	Colin Blakely
Bullock, a country clown	James Mellor
Costar Pearmain ⎫ two recruits	John Stride
Thomas Appletree ⎭	Keith Marsh
Bridewell, a constable	Michael Rothwell
Pluck, a butcher	Trevor Martin
Thomas, a smith	Dan Meaden
A Poacher	Clive Rust
A Collier	Richard Hampton
Drummer	Alan Ridgway
Boy with whistle	Christopher Chittell
Balance's steward	Rod Beacham
Melinda's servant	Mike Gambon
Melinda, a lady of fortune	Mary Miller
Silvia, daughter of Balance, in love with Plume	Maggie Smith
Lucy, Melinda's maid	Jeanne Hepple
Rose, a country wench	Lynn Redgrave
Poacher's wife	Jeanette Landis
Collier's wife	Elizabeth Burger

Production by William Gaskill

Scenery and Costumes by René Allio
Music arranged by Richard Hampton

The Scene: Shrewsbury, 1705

Lighting by Richard Pilbrow
Assistant to the Producer: Desmond O'Donovan

Dramatis Personae

MEN

MR BALANCE	
MR SCALE	Three Justices
MR SCRUPLE	
MR WORTHY	A Gentleman of Shropshire
CAPTAIN PLUME	
CAPTAIN BRAZEN	Two Recruiting Officers
KITE	Sergeant to Plume
BULLOCK	A Country Clown
COSTAR PEARMAIN	
THOMAS APPLETREE	Two Recruits
PLUCK	A Butcher
THOMAS	A Smith

WOMEN

MELINDA	A Lady of Fortune
SILVIA	Daughter to Balance, in love with Plume
LUCY	Melinda's maid
ROSE	A Country Wench

Constable, Recruits, Mob, Servants, and Attendants etc.

SCENE: SHREWSBURY

Prologue

In ancient times, when Helen's fatal charms
Roused the contending universe to arms,
The Grecian council happily deputes
The sly Ulysses forth—to raise recruits.
The artful captain found, without delay,
Where great Achilles, a deserter, lay.
Him Fate hath warn'd to shun the Trojan
   blows:
Him Greece required—against their Trojan
   foes.
All the recruiting arts were needful here
To raise this great, this tim'rous volunteer.
Ulysses well could talk: he stirs, he warms
The warlike youth. He listens to the charms
Of plunder, fine laced coats, and glitt'ring
   arms.
Ulysses caught the young aspiring boy,
And listed him who wrought the fate of
   Troy.
Thus by recruiting was bold Hector slain:
Recruiting thus fair Helen did regain.
If for one Helen such prodigious things
Were acted, that they even listed kings;
If for one Helen's artful, vicious charms,
Half the transported world was found in
   arms
What for so many Helens may we dare,
Whose minds, as well as faces, are so fair?
If by one Helen's eyes old Greece could find
Its Homer fired to write—even Homer blind;
The Britons sure beyond compare may
   write,
That view so many Helens every night.

The audience enters to find the curtain up, revealing a formal, symmetrical setting of moss-green panels. Before the action starts, the panels revolve, and the setting becomes rustic, informal and asymmetrical.

The townsfolk's only reaction to Kite's *spiel* is suspicious silence: they have been had before.

Pearmain: not a dumb ox, but the shrewdest of the local boys—an important and difficult victim for Kite to entrap.

Act One

SCENE ONE

Enter DRUMMER, *beating the 'Grenadier's March'*, SERGEANT KITE, COSTAR PEARMAIN, THOMAS APPLETREE *and* MOB *following*.

KITE: (*making a speech*) If any gentlemen soldiers, or others, have a mind to serve her Majesty, and pull down the French king: if any prentices have severe masters, any children have undutiful parents: if any servants have too little wages, or any husband too much wife: let them repair to the noble Sergeant Kite, at the sign of the Raven in this good town of Shrewsbury and they shall receive present relief and entertainment.—Gentlemen, I don't beat my drums here to ensnare or inveigle any man; for you must know, gentlemen, that I am a man of honour. Besides, I don't beat up for common soldiers; no, I list only grenadiers —grenadiers, gentlemen. Pray, gentlemen, observe this cap. This is the cap of honour, it dubs a man a gentleman in the drawing of a trigger; and he that has the good fortune to be born six foot high, was born to be a great man.—(*To* COSTAR PEARMAIN) Sir, will you give me leave to try this cap upon your head?

PEARMAIN: Is there no harm in't? Won't the cap list me?

KITE: No, no, no more than I can.—Come, let me see how it becomes you?

PEARMAIN: Are you sure there be no conjuration in it? no gunpowder plot upon me?

KITE: No, no, friend; don't fear, man.

PEARMAIN: My mind misgives me plaguily. —Let me see it. (*Going to put it on*) It smells

20

woundily of sweat and brimstone. Pray, sergeant, what writing is this upon the face of it?

KITE: The Crown, or the Bed of Honour.

PEARMAIN: Pray now, what may be that same bed of honour?

KITE: Oh! a mighty large bed! bigger by half than the great bed of Ware—ten thousand people may lie in it together, and never feel one another.

PEARMAIN: My wife and I would do well to lie in't, for we don't care for feeling one another.—But do folk sleep sound in this same bed of honour?

KITE: Sound! Ay, so sound that they never wake.

PEARMAIN: Wauns! I wish again that my wife lay there.

KITE: Say you so? then, I find, brother—

PEARMAIN: Brother! Hold there, friend; I am no kindred to you that I know of yet. Look'ee, sergeant, no coaxing, no wheedling, d'ye see: If I have a mind to list, why so; if not, why 'tis not so; therefore take your cap and your brothership back again, for I an't disposed at this present writing.— No coaxing, no brothering me, faith!

KITE: I coax! I wheedle! I'm above it! Sir, I have served twenty campaigns. But, sir, you talk well, and I must own that you are a man every inch of you, a pretty young sprightly fellow. I love a fellow with a spirit; but I scorn to coax, 'tis base: though I must say, that never in my life have I seen a man better built; how firm and strong he treads! he steps like a castle; but I scorn to wheedle any man.—Come, honest lad, will you take share of a pot?

PEARMAIN: Nay, for that matter, I'll spend my penny with the best he that wears a head, that is, begging your pardon, sir, and in a fair way.

KITE: Give me your hand then; and now, gentlemen, I have no more to say, but this— here's a purse of gold, and there is a tub of humming ale at my quarters! 'tis the queen's money, and the queen's drink.—She's a generous queen, and loves her subjects— I hope, gentlemen, you won't refuse the queen's health?

MOB: No, no, no!

KITE: Huzza then! huzza for the queen, and the honour of Shropshire!

MOB: Huzza!

KITE: Beat drum.

Exeunt, DRUMMER beating the 'Grenadier's March'.
Enter PLUME in a riding habit.

PLUME: By the Grenadier March, that should be my drum, and by that shout, it should beat with success.—Let me see— (*Looking on his watch*)—four o'clock. At ten yesterday morning I left London. A hundred and twenty miles in thirty hours is

Kite's relationship with Plume is close and not unduly deferential. The news about Molly's bastard is delivered quite deadpan: as is the list of Kite's five wives.

pretty smart riding, but nothing to the fatigue of recruiting.

Re-enter KITE.

KITE: Welcome to Shrewsbury, noble Captain! From the banks of the Danube to the Severn side, noble Captain, you're welcome!

PLUME: A very elegant reception indeed, Mr Kite! I find you are fairly entered into your recruiting strain. Pray, what success?

KITE: I have been here but a week, and I have recruited five.

PLUME: Five! Pray what are they?

KITE: I have listed the strong man of Kent, the king of the gipsies, a Scotch pedlar, a scoundrel attorney, and a Welsh parson.

PLUME: An attorney! Wert thou mad? List a lawyer? Discharge him, discharge him this minute.

KITE: Why sir?

PLUME: Because I will have nobody in my company that can write; a fellow that can write, can draw petitions.—I say this minute discharge him.

KITE: And what shall I do with the parson?

PLUME: Can he write?

KITE: Hum! He plays rarely upon the fiddle.

PLUME: Keep him by all means.—But how stands the country affected? Were the people pleased with the news of my coming to town?

KITE: Sir, the mob are so pleased with your honour, and the justices and better sort of people are so delighted with me, that we shall soon do our business.—But, sir, you have got a recruit here that you little think of.

PLUME: Who?

KITE: One that you beat up for last time you were in the country: you remember your old friend Molly at the Castle?

PLUME: She's not with child, I hope?

KITE: No, no, sir—she was brought to bed yesterday.

PLUME: Kite, you must father the child.

KITE: And so her friends will oblige me to marry the mother.

PLUME: If they should, we'll take her with us; she can wash, you know, and make a bed upon occasion.

KITE: Ay, or unmake it upon occasion. But your honour knows that I am married already.

PLUME: To how many?

KITE: I can't tell readily—I have set them down here upon the back of the muster-roll.—(*Draws it out*) Let me see,—Imprimis, Mrs Sheely Snikereyes; she sells potatoes upon Ormond Quay in Dublin—Peggy Guzzle, the brandy-woman, at the Horse-Guard at Whitehall—Dolly Waggon, the carrier's daughter at Hull—Mademoiselle Van-Bottomflat at the Buss.—Then Jenny Oakam, the ship-carpenter's widow, at Portsmouth; but I don't reckon upon her, for she was married at the same time to two lieutenants of marines, and a man-of-war's boatswain.

PLUME: A full company!—You have named five—come, make 'em half-a-dozen, Kite. Is the child a boy or a girl?

KITE: A chopping boy.

PLUME: Then set the mother down in your list, and the boy in mine. Enter him a grenadier by the name of Francis Kite, absent upon furlough. I'll allow you a man's pay for his subsistence; and now go comfort the wench in the straw.

KITE: I shall, sir.

PLUME: But hold; have you made any use of your German doctor's habit since you arrived?

KITE: Yes, yes, sir, and my fame's all about the country for the most faithful fortune-teller that ever told a lie.—I was obliged to let my landlord into the secret, for the convenience of keeping it so; but he's an honest fellow, and will be faithful to any roguery that is trusted to him. This device, sir, will get you men and me money, which I think, is all we want at present.—But yonder comes your friend Mr Worthy.—Has your honour any farther commands?

PLUME: None at present.—(*Exit* KITE) 'Tis indeed the picture of Worthy, but the life's departed.

Enter WORTHY.

What! Arms a-cross, Worthy! Methinks, you should hold 'em open when a friend's so near.—The man has got the vapours in his ears I believe: I must expel this melancholy spirit.

    Spleen, thou worst of fiends below,
    Fly, I conjure thee by this magic blow.

Slaps WORTHY *on the shoulder.*

WORTHY: Plume! my dear Captain, welcome. Safe and sound returned?

PLUME: I 'scaped safe from Germany, and sound, I hope, from London; you see I have lost neither leg, arm, nor nose. Then for my inside, 'tis neither troubled with sympathies nor antipathies; and I have an excellent stomach for roast-beef.

WORTHY: Thou art a happy fellow; once I was so.

PLUME: What ails thee, man? No inundations nor earthquakes in Wales, I hope? Has your father rose from the dead, and reassumed his estate?

WORTHY: No.

PLUME: Then you are married, surely?

WORTHY: No.

PLUME: Then you are mad, or turning Quaker?

WORTHY: Come, I must out with it.—Your once gay, roving friend is dwindled into an obsequious, thoughtful, romantic, constant coxcomb.

PLUME: And, pray, what is all this for?

WORTHY: For a woman.

PLUME: Shake hands, brother; if you go to that, behold me as obsequious, as thoughtful, and as constant a coxcomb as your worship.

WORTHY: For whom?

PLUME: For a regiment.—But for a woman! —'Sdeath! I have been constant to fifteen at a time, but never melancholy for one; and can the love of one bring you into this pickle? Pray, who is this miraculous Helen?

WORTHY: A Helen indeed, not to be won under a ten years' siege: as great a beauty, and as great a jilt.

PLUME: A jilt! Pho! Is she as great a whore?

WORTHY: No, no.

PLUME: 'Tis ten thousand pities. But who is she? Do I know her?

WORTHY: Very well.

PLUME: Impossible!—I know no woman that will hold out a ten years' siege.

WORTHY: What think you of Melinda?

PLUME: Melinda! Why, she began to capitulate this time twelvemonth, and offered to surrender upon honourable terms; and I advised you to propose a settlement of five hundred pounds a year to her, before I went last abroad.

WORTHY: I did, and she hearkened to't, desiring only one week to consider: when, beyond her hopes, the town was relieved, and I forced to turn my siege into a blockade.

PLUME: Explain, explain!

WORTHY: My lady Richly, her aunt in Flintshire, dies, and leaves her, at this critical time, twenty thousand pounds.

PLUME: Oh! the devil! What a delicate woman was there spoiled! But, by the rules of war now, Worthy, blockade was foolish. After such a convoy of provisions was entered the place, you could have no thought of reducing it by famine; you should have redoubled your attacks, taken the town by storm, or have died upon the breach.

WORTHY: I did make one general assault, and pushed it with all my forces; but I was so vigorously repulsed, that, despairing of ever gaining her for a mistress, I have altered my conduct, given my addresses the obsequious and distant turn, and court her now for a wife.

PLUME: So as you grew obsequious, she grew haughty; and because you approached her as a goddess, she used you like a dog?

WORTHY: Exactly.

PLUME: 'Tis the way of 'em all. Come, Worthy, your obsequious and distant airs will never bring you together; you must not think to surmount her pride by your humility.

Would you bring her to better thoughts of you, she must be reduced to a meaner opinion of herself. Let me see: the very first thing that I would do, should be to lie with her chamber-maid, and hire three or four wenches in the neighbourhood to report that I had got them with child. Suppose we lampooned all the pretty women in town, and left her out? Or what if we made a ball, and forgot to invite her, with one or two of the ugliest?

WORTHY: These would be mortifications, I must confess; but we live in such a precise, dull place, that we can have no balls, no lampoons, no—

PLUME: What! no bastards! and so many recruiting officers in town! I thought 'twas a maxim among them to leave as many recruits in the country as they carried out.

WORTHY: Nobody doubts your good-will, noble captain, in serving your country with your best blood; witness our friend Molly at the Castle. There have been tears in town about that business, Captain.

PLUME: I hope Silvia has not heard of't?

WORTHY: O sir, have you thought of her? I began to fancy you had forgot poor Silvia.

PLUME: Your affairs had put mine quite out of my head. 'Tis true, Silvia and I had once agreed to go to bed together, could we have adjusted preliminaries; but she would have the wedding before consummation, and I was for consummation before the wedding; we could not agree. She was a pert, obstinate fool, and would lose her maidenhead her own way; so she may keep it for Plume.

WORTHY: But do you intend to marry upon no other conditions?

PLUME: Your pardon, sir, I'll marry upon no condition at all. If I should, I am resolved never to bind myself to a woman for my whole life, till I know whether I shall like her company for half an hour. Suppose I

Performed as follows, with a modern *double entente* added:

WORTHY: '... we can have no balls—'

PLUME: *'What?'*

WORTHY: 'no *lampoons*. ...'

married a woman that wanted a leg!—such a thing might be, unless I examined the goods beforehand. If people would but try one another's constitutions before they engaged, it would prevent all these elopements, divorces, and the devil knows what.

WORTHY: Nay, for that matter, the town did not stick to say, that—

PLUME: I hate country towns for that reason. If your town has a dishonourable thought of Silvia it deserves to be burned to the ground. I love Silvia, I admire her frank, generous disposition. There's something in that girl more than woman. Her sex is but a foil to her—the ingratitude, dissimulation, envy, pride, avarice, and vanity of her sister females, do but set off their contraries in her. In short, were I once a general, I would marry her.

WORTHY: Faith, you have reason; for were you but a corporal she would marry you. But my Melinda coquettes it with every fellow she sees. I'll lay fifty pound she makes love to you.

PLUME: I'll lay fifty pound that I return it, if she does. Look'ee, Worthy, I'll win her, and give her to you afterwards.

WORTHY: If you win her you shall wear her. Faith, I would not value the conquest without the credit of the victory.

Re-enter KITE.

KITE: Captain, captain, a word in your ear.

PLUME: You may speak out, here are none but friends.

KITE: You know, sir, that you sent me to comfort the good woman in the straw, Mrs Molly—my wife, Mr Worthy.

WORTHY: O ho! Very well! I wish you joy, Mr Kite.

KITE: Your worship very well may, for I have got both a wife and a child in half-an-hour. But, as I was saying, you sent me to comfort Mrs Molly—my wife, I mean—but what d'ye think, sir? She was better comforted before I came.

PLUME: As how?

KITE: Why, sir, a footman in a blue livery had brought her ten guineas to buy her baby-clothes.

PLUME: Who, in the name of wonder, could send them?

KITE: Nay, sir, I must whisper that (*Whispers*)—Mrs Silvia.

PLUME: Silvia! generous creature!

WORTHY: Silvia! impossible!

KITE: Here be the guineas, sir; I took the gold as part of my wife's portion. Nay, farther, sir, she sent word the child should be taken all imaginable care of, and that she intended to stand godmother. The same footman, as I was coming to you with this news, called after me, and told me, that his lady would speak with me. I went, and, upon hearing that you were come to town, she gave me half-a-guinea for the news; and ordered me to tell you that Justice Balance, her father, who is just come out of the country, would be glad to see you.

PLUME: There's a girl for you, Worthy! Is there anything of woman in this? No, 'tis noble, generous, manly friendship. Show me another woman that would lose an inch of her prerogative, that way, without tears, fits, and reproaches! The common jealousy of her sex, which is nothing but their avarice of pleasure, she despises; and can part with the lover, though she dies for the man. —Come, Worthy: where's the best wine? for there I'll quarter.

WORTHY: Horton has a fresh pipe of choice Barcelona, which I would not let him pierce before, because I reserved the maidenhead of it for your welcome to town.

PLUME: Let's away then.—Mr Kite, wait on the lady with my humble service, and tell her I shall only refresh a little, and wait upon her.

WORTHY: Hold, Kite!—Have you seen the other recruiting-captain?

KITE: No, sir.

PLUME: Another! who is he?

WORTHY; My rival in the first place, and the most unaccountable fellow but I'll tell you more as we go.

Exeunt.

Act One

SCENE TWO

MELINDA's *apartment.*
MELINDA *and* SILVIA *meeting.*

MELINDA: Welcome to town, cousin Silvia —(*Salute*). I envied you your retreat in the country; for Shrewsbury, methinks, and all your heads of shires, are the most irregular places for living. Here we have smoke, noise, scandal, affectation, and pretensions; in short, everything to give the spleen—and nothing to divert it. Then the air is intolerable.

SILVIA: O madam! I have heard the town commended for its air.

MELINDA: But you don't consider, Silvia, how long I have lived in't! for I can assure you, that to a lady, the least nice in her constitution, no air can be good above half a year. Change of air I take to be the most agreeable of any variety in life.

SILVIA: As you say, cousin Melinda, there are several sorts of airs.

MELINDA: Psha! I talk only of the air we breathe, or more properly of that we taste. Have you not, Silvia, found a vast difference in the taste of airs?

SILVIA: Pray, cousin, are not vapours a sort of air? Taste air! You might as well tell me, I may feed upon air. But prithee, my dear Melinda, don't put on such an air to me. Your education and mine were just the same; and I remember the time when we never troubled our heads about air, but when the sharp air from the Welsh mountains made our fingers ache in a cold morning at the boarding-school.

MELINDA: Our education, cousin, was the same, but our temperaments had nothing alike; you have the constitution of a horse.

SILVIA: So far as to be troubled with neither spleen, colic, nor vapours. I need no salts for my stomach, no hartshorn for my head, nor wash for my complexion; I can gallop all the morning after the hunting-horn, and all the evening after a fiddle. In short, I can do everything with my father, but drink, and shoot flying; and I am sure, I can do everything my mother could, were I put to the trial.

MELINDA: You are in a fair way of being put to't; for I am told your captain is come to town.

SILVIA: Ay, Melinda, he is come; and I'll take care he shan't go without a companion.

MELINDA: You are certainly mad, cousin!

SILVIA: And there's a pleasure in being mad, which none but madmen know.

MELINDA: Thou poor romantic Quixote! Hast thou the vanity to imagine that a young sprightly officer, that rambles o'er half the globe in half a year, can confine his thoughts to the little daughter of a country justice, in an obscure part of the world?

SILVIA: Psha! What care I for his thoughts? I should not like a man with confined thoughts, it shows a narrowness of soul. Constancy is but a dull sleepy quality at best, they will hardly admit it among the manly virtues; nor do I think it deserves a place with bravery, knowledge, policy, justice, and some other qualities that are proper to that noble sex. In short, Melinda, I think a petticoat a mighty simple thing, and I am heartily tired of my sex.

MELINDA: That is, you are tired of an

appendix to our sex, that you can't so handsomely get rid of in petticoats, as if you were in breeches. O' my conscience, Silvia, hadst thou been a man, thou hadst been the greatest rake in Christendom.

SILVIA: I should have endeavoured to know the world, which a man can never do thoroughly without half a hundred friend-ships, and as many amours. But now I think on't, how stands your affair with Mr Worthy?

MELINDA: He's my aversion!

SILVIA: Vapours!

MELINDA: What do you say, madam?

SILVIA: I say, that you should not use that honest fellow so inhumanly. He's a gentle-man of parts and fortune; and besides that, he's my Plume's friend, and by all that's sacred, if you don't use him better, I shall expect satisfaction.

MELINDA: Satisfaction! You begin to fancy yourself in breeches in good earnest. But to be plain with you, I like Worthy the worse for being so intimate with your captain, for I take him to be a loose, idle, unmannerly coxcomb.

SILVIA: O madam! You never saw him, per-haps, since you were mistress of twenty-thousand pounds; you only knew him when you were capitulating with Worthy for a settlement, which perhaps might encourage him to be a little loose and unmannerly with you.

MELINDA: What do you mean, madam?

SILVIA: My meaning needs no interpreta-tion, madam.

MELINDA: Better it had, madam; for me-thinks you are too plain.

SILVIA: If you mean the plainness of my person, I think your ladyship's as plain as me to the full.

MELINDA: Were I sure of that, I should be glad to take up with a rakehelly officer, as you do.

SILVIA: Again!—Look'ee, madam, you're in your own house.

MELINDA: And if you had kept in yours, I should have excused you.

SILVIA: Don't be troubled, madam, I shan'n't desire to have my visit returned.

MELINDA: The sooner, therefore, you make an end of this the better.

SILVIA: I am easily persuaded to follow my inclinations, so, madam, your humble servant. (*Exit*)

MELINDA: Saucy thing!

Enter LUCY.

LUCY: What's the matter, madam!

MELINDA: Did you not see the proud nothing, how she swelled upon the arrival of her fellow?

LUCY: Her fellow has not been long enough arrived to occasion any great swelling, madam; I don't believe she has seen him yet.

MELINDA: Nor sha'n't if I can help it.—Let me see—I have it! Bring me pen and ink.—Hold, I'll go write in my closet.

LUCY: An answer to this letter, I hope, madam. (*Presents a letter*)

MELINDA: Who sent it?

LUCY: Your captain, madam.

MELINDA: He's a fool, and I am tired of him. Send it back unopened.

LUCY: The messenger's gone, madam.

MELINDA: Then how should I send an answer? Call him back immediately, while I go write.

Exeunt.

After Melinda's exit, Lucy kisses the letter and tucks it in her bosom—thus planting her love of Brazen, never very satisfactorily established in the text, though it plays a crucial part in the *dénouement*.

Act Two

SCENE ONE

An apartment in Justice BALANCE's *house.*
Enter Justice BALANCE *and* PLUME.

BALANCE: Look'ee, Captain, give us but blood for our money, and you sha'n't want men. I remember that, for some years of the last war, we had no blood nor wounds, but in the officers mouths; nothing for our millions but newspapers not worth a reading. Our armies did nothing but play at prison bars and hide-and-seek with the enemy; but now ye have brought us colours, and standards, and prisoners. Ad's my life, Captain, get us but another Marshal of France, and I'll go myself for a soldier.

PLUME: Pray, Mr Balance, how does your fair daughter?

BALANCE: Ah, Captain! What is my daughter to a Marshal of France? We're upon a nobler subject, I want to have a particular description of the battle of Hockstat.

PLUME: The battle, sir, was a very pretty battle as one should desire to see, but we were all so intent upon victory, that we never minded the battle. All that I know of the matter is, our general commanded us to beat the French, and we did so; and if he pleases but to say the word, we'll do't again. But pray, sir, how does Mrs Silvia?

BALANCE: Still upon Silvia! For shame, Captain! You are engaged already, wedded to the war. Victory is your mistress, and 'tis below a soldier to think of any other.

PLUME: As a mistress, I confess, but as a friend, Mr Balance.

BALANCE: Come, come, Captain, never mince the matter: would not you debauch

my daughter if you could?

PLUME: How, sir! I hope she's not to be debauched.

BALANCE: Faith, but she is, sir; and any woman in England of her age and complexion, by a man of your youth and vigour. Look'ee, Captain, once I was young, and once an officer as you are; and I can guess at your thoughts now, by what mine were then; and I remember very well, that I would have given one of my legs to have deluded the daughter of an old plain country gentlemen, as like me as I was then like you.

PLUME: But, sir, was that country gentleman your friend and benefactor?

BALANCE: Not much of that.

PLUME: There the comparison breaks: the favours, sir, that—

BALANCE: Pho, I hate speeches! If I have done you any service, Captain, 'twas to please myself, for I love thee; and if I could part with my girl, you should have her as soon as any young fellow I know. But I hope you have more honour than to quit the service, and she more prudence than to follow the camp; but she's at her own disposal, she has fifteen hundred pound in her pocket; and so—Silvia, Silvia!

Enter SILVIA.

SILVIA: There are some letters, sir, come by the post from London; I left them upon the table in your closet.

BALANCE: And here is a gentleman from Germany—(*Presents* PLUME *to her*) Captain, you'll excuse me, I'll go read my letters, and wait on you. (*Exit*)

SILVIA: Sir you are welcome to England.

PLUME: You are indebted to me a welcome, madam, since the hopes of receiving it from this fair hand was the principal cause of my seeing England.

SILVIA: I have often heard that soldiers were sincere; shall I venture to believe

public report?

PLUME: You may, when 'tis backed by private insurance: for I swear, madam, by the honour of my profession, that whatever dangers I went upon, it was with the hope of making myself more worthy of your esteem; and, if ever I had thoughts of preserving my life, 'twas for the pleasure of dying at your feet.

SILVIA: Well, well, you shall die at my feet, or where you will; but you know, sir, there is a certain will and testament to be made beforehand.

PLUME: My will, madam, is made already, and there it is (*Gives her a parchment*); and if you please to open that parchment, which was drawn the evening before the battle of Blenheim, you will find whom I left my heir.

SILVIA: (*Opens the will and reads*) Mrs Silvia Balance.—Well, Captain, this is a handsome and a substantial compliment; but I can assure you, I am much better pleased with the bare knowledge of your intention, than I should have been in the possession of your legacy. But methinks, sir, you should have left something to your little boy at the Castle.

PLUME: (*Aside*) That's home!—(*Aloud*) My little boy! Lack-a-day, madam, that alone may convince you 'twas none of mine. Why the girl, madam, is my serjeant's wife, and so the poor creature gave out that I was father, in hopes that my friends might support her in case of necessity—that was all, madam.—My boy! no, no, no.

Enter a SERVANT.

SERVANT: Madam, my master has received some ill news from London, and desires to speak with you immediately, and he begs the Captain's pardon, that he can't wait on him as he promised. (*Exit*)

PLUME: Ill news! Heavens avert it! Nothing could touch me nearer than to see that generous worthy gentleman afflicted. I'll leave you to comfort him; and be assured, that if my life and fortune can be any way serviceable to the father of my Silvia, he shall freely command both.

SILVIA: The necessity must be very pressing that would engage me to endanger either.

Exeunt severally.

Act Two

SCENE TWO

Another apartment.
Enter BALANCE and SILVIA.

SILVIA: Whilst there is life there is hopes, sir; perhaps my brother may recover.

BALANCE: We have but little reason to expect it; Doctor Kilman acquaints me here, that before this comes to my hands, he fears I shall have no son. Poor Owen!— But the decree is just: I was pleased with the death of my father, because he left me an estate, and now I'm punished with the loss of an heir to inherit mine. I must now look upon you as the only hopes of my family; and I expect that the augmentation of your fortune will give you fresh thoughts, and new prospects.

SILVIA: My desire of being punctual in my obedience, requires that you would be plain in your commands, sir.

BALANCE: The death of your brother makes you sole heiress to my estate, which you know is about twelve hundred pounds a year. This fortune gives you a fair claim to quality, and a title; you must set a just value upon yourself, and, in plain term, think no more of Captain Plume.

SILVIA: You have often commended the gentleman, sir.

BALANCE: And I do so still; he's a very pretty fellow. But though I liked him well enough for a bare son-in-law, I don't approve of him for an heir to my estate and family. Fifteen hundred pounds indeed I might trust in his hands, and it might do the young fellow a kindness; but od's my life! twelve hundred pounds a year would ruin him—quite turn his brain! A captain of foot worthy twelve hundred pounds a year! 'tis a prodigy in nature. Besides this, I have five or six thousand pounds in woods upon my estate; oh, that would make him stark mad! For you must know that all captains have a mighty aversion to timber; they can't endure to see trees standing. Then I should have some rogue of a builder, by the help of his damned magic art, transform my noble oaks and elms into cornices, portals, sashes, birds, beasts, and devils, to adorn some maggotty, new-fashioned bauble upon the Thames; and then you should have a dog of a gardener bring a habeas corpus for my terra firma, remove it to Chelsea or Twittenham, and clap it into grass-plats and gravel-walks.

Enter a SERVANT.

SERVANT: Sir, here's one below with a letter for your worship, but he will deliver it into no hands but your own.

BALANCE: Come, show me the messenger.

Exit with SERVANT.

SILVIA: Make the dispute between love and duty, and I am prince Prettyman exactly. If my brother dies, ah poor brother! If he lives, ah poor sister! 'Tis bad both ways; I'll try it again. Follow my own inclinations, and break my father's heart; or obey his commands, and break my own? Worse and worse. Suppose I take it thus?—a moderate fortune, a pretty fellow, and a nag; or a fine estate, a coach-and-six, and an ass. That will never do neither.

Re-enter BALANCE *and* SERVANT.

BALANCE: (*To* SERVANT) Put four horses into the coach. (*Exit* SERVANT) Ho, Silvia!

SILVIA: Sir.

BALANCE: How old were you when your mother died?

SILVIA: So young that I don't remember I ever had one; and you have been so careful, so indulgent to me since, that indeed I never wanted one.

BALANCE: Have I ever denied you anything you asked of me?

SILVIA: Never that I remember.

BALANCE: Then, Silvia, I must beg that, once in your life, you would grant me a favour.

SILVIA: Why should you question it, sir?

BALANCE: I don't; but I would rather counsel than command. I don't propose this with the authority of a parent, but as the advice of your friend: that you would take the coach this moment, and go into the country.

SILVIA: Does this advice, sir, proceed from the contents of the letter you received just now?

This promise—and Silvia's determination to keep to the letter of it—motivates everything she does in what follows: e.g. she volunteers for the army in breeches in order to make Balance 'dispose of' her to Plume.

BALANCE: No matter; I will be with you in three or four days, and then give you my reasons. But before you go, I expect you will make me one solemn promise.

SILVIA: Propose the thing, sir.

BALANCE: That you will never dispose of yourself to any man without my consent.

SILVIA: I promise.

BALANCE: Very well; and to be even with you, I promise that I will never dispose of you without your own consent. And so, Silvia, the coach is ready; farewell!—(*Leads her to the door, and returns*). Now she's gone, I'll examine the contents of this letter a little nearer. (*Reads*)

Sir,

My intimacy with Mr Worthy has drawn a secret from him that he had from his friend Captain Plume; and my friendship and relation to your family oblige me to give you timely notice of it: the Captain has dishonourable designs upon my cousin Silvia. Evils of this nature are more easily prevented than amended; and that you would immediately send my cousin into the country, is the advice of, sir, your humble servant, MELINDA.

Why, the devil's in the young fellows of this age! They are ten times worse than they were in my time. Had he made my daughter a whore, and forswore it like a gentleman, I could have almost pardoned it; but to tell tales beforehand is monstrous. Hang it, I can fetch down a woodcock or a snipe, and why not a hat and feather? I have a case of good pistols, and have a good mind to try.

Enter WORTHY.

Worthy, your servant.

WORTHY: I'm sorry, sir, to be the messenger of ill news.

BALANCE: I apprehend it, sir: you have heard that my son Owen is past recovery.

WORTHY: My letters say he's dead, sir.

BALANCE: He's happy, and I'm satisfied.

The strokes of Heaven I can bear; but injuries from men, Mr Worthy, are not so easily supported.

WORTHY: I hope, sir, you're under no apprehension of wrong from anybody?

BALANCE: You know I ought to be.

WORTHY: You wrong my honour, sir, in believing I could know anything to your prejudice without resenting it as much as you should.

BALANCE: This letter, sir, which I tear in pieces to conceal the person that sent it, informs me that Plume has a design upon Silvia, and that you are privy to't. (*Tears the letter*)

WORTHY: Nay then, sir, I must do myself justice, and endeavour to find out the author.—(*Takes up a fragment of the letter*) Sir, I know the hand, and if you refuse to discover the contents, Melinda shall tell me. (*Going*)

BALANCE: Hold, sir! The contents I have told you already, only with this circumstance, that her intimacy with Mr Worthy has drawn the secret from him.

WORTHY: Her intimacy with me!—Dear sir, let me pick up the pieces of this letter; 'twill give me such a power over her pride, to have her own an intimacy under her hand.—(*Gathering up the letter*) 'Twas the luckiest accident! The aspersion, sir, was nothing but malice, the effect of a little quarrel between her and Mrs Silvia.

BALANCE: Are you sure of that, sir?

WORTHY: Her maid gave me the history of part of the battle just now, as she overheard it. But I hope, sir, your daughter has suffered nothing upon the account?

BALANCE: No, no, poor girl; she's so afflicted with the news of her brother's death, that to avoid company she begged leave to be gone into the country.

WORTHY: And is she gone?

BALANCE: I could not refuse her, she was so pressing; the coach went from the door the minute before you came.

WORTHY: So pressing to be gone, sir! I find her fortune will give her the same airs with Melinda, and then Plume and I may laugh at one another.

BALANCE: Like enough; women are as subject to pride as we are, and why mayn't great women, as well as great men, forget their old acquaintance? But come, where's this young fellow? I love him so well, it would break the heart of me to think him a rascal.—(*Aside*) I'm glad my daughter's gone fairly off, though.—(*Aloud*) Where does the captain quarter?

WORTHY: At Horton's; I am to meet him there two hours hence, and we should be glad of your company.

BALANCE: Your pardon, dear Worthy; I must allow a day or two to the death of my son; the decorum of mourning is what we owe the world, because they pay it to us. Afterwards, I'm yours over a bottle, or how you will.

WORTHY: Sir, I'm your humble servant.

Exeunt severally.

Act Two

SCENE THREE

The street.
Enter KITE *leading* COSTAR PEARMAIN *in one hand, and* THOMAS APPLETREE *in the other, both drunk.*
KITE *sings.*

KITE: Our prentice Tom may now refuse
        To wipe his scoundrel master's
          shoes;
        For now he's free to sing and play—
        Over the hills and far away,
        Over the hills, etc. (PEARMAIN *and*
          APPLETREE *sing the Chorus*)

        We all shall lead more happy lives
        By getting rid of brats and wives,
        That scold and brawl both night and
          day—
        Over the hills and far away.
        Over the hills, etc.

Hey, boys! thus we soldiers live; drink, sing, dance, play! We live, as one should say—we live—'tis impossible to tell how we live. We are all princes. Why—why, you are a king, you are an emperor, and I'm a prince. Now, ain't we—

APPLETREE: No, serjeant, I'll be no emperor.

KITE: No!

APPLETREE: No, I'll be a justice of peace.

KITE: A justice of peace, man!

APPLETREE: Ay, wauns will I; for since this Pressing Act, they are greater than any emperor under the sun.

KITE: Done! You are a justice of peace, and you are a king, and I am a duke; and a rum

Plume's arrival is not fortuitous: he enters at a signal from Kite.

duke, an't I?

PEARMAIN: Ay, but I'll be no king.

KITE: What then?

PEARMAIN: I'll be a queen.

KITE: A queen!

PEARMAIN: Ay, Queen of England; that's greater than any king of 'em all.

KITE: Bravely said, faith! Huzza for the Queen!—(*Huzza*) But heark'ee, you Mr Justice, and you Mr Queen, did you ever see the Queen's picture?

BOTH: No, no, no.

KITE: I wonder at that; I have two of 'em set in gold, and as like her Majesty, God bless the mark!—See here, they are set in gold.

Takes two broad pieces out of his pocket, and gives one to each

APPLETREE: The wonderful works of Nature! (*Looking at it*)

PEARMAIN: What's this written about? Here's a posy, I believe,—Ca-ro-lus.—What's that, serjeant?

KITE: Oh, Carolus!—Why, Carolus is Latin for Queen Anne,—that's all.

PEARMAIN: 'Tis a fine thing to be a scollard!—Serjeant, will you part with this? I'll buy it on you, if it come within the compass of a crown.

KITE: A crown! Never talk of buying; 'tis the same thing among friends, you know; I'll present them to ye both; you shall give me as good a thing. Put 'em up, and remember your old friend, when I am over the hills and far away?

*They sing and put up the money
Enter PLUME, singing*

PLUME: Over the hills and o'er the main
        To Flanders, Portugal, or Spain:
        The queen commands, and we'll
          obey—
        Over the hills and far away.

Come on, my men of mirth, away with it

Kite places Pearmain and Appletree back to back.

I'll make one among ye.—Who are these hearty lads?

KITE: Off with your hats; 'ounds, off with your hats! This is the captain, the captain.

APPLETREE: We have sen captains afore now, mun.

PEARMAIN: Ay, and lieutenant-captains too; flesh, I'se keep on my nab!

APPLETREE: And I'se scarcely doff mine for any captain in England. My vether's a freeholder.

PLUME: Who are these jolly lads, serjeant?

KITE: A couple of honest brave fellows, that are willing to serve the Queen: I have entertained 'em just now, as volunteers, under your honour's command.

PLUME: And good entertainment they shall have. Volunteers are the men I want, those are the men fit to make soldiers, captains, generals!

PEARMAIN: Wauns, Tummas, what's this! Are you listed?

APPLETREE: Flesh, not I: are you, Costar?

PEARMAIN: Wauns, not I!

KITE: What, not listed! Ha, ha, ha! a very good jest, faith!

PEARMAIN: Come, Tummas, we'll go home.

APPLETREE: Ay, ay, come.

KITE: Home! for shame, gentlemen, behave yourselves better before your captain! Dear Tummas, honest Costar—

APPLETREE: No, no, we'll be gone.

KITE: Nay then, I command you to stay: I place you both sentinels in this place for two hours: to watch the motion of St Mary's clock, you; and you the motion of St Chad's. And he that dares stir from his post till he be relieved, shall have my sword in his guts the next minute.

PLUME: What's the matter, serjeant? I'm afraid you are too rough with these gentle-

During rehearsals Kite improvised as follows: "... and they should both be shot as an example to one another." This impromptu—a distinct improvement on Farquhar's original—was retained in performance.

men.

KITE: I'm too mild, sir: they disobey command, sir, and one of 'em should be shot for an example to the other.

PEARMAIN: Shot, Tummas!

PLUME: Come, gentlemen, what's the matter?

PEARMAIN: We don't know; the noble serjeant is pleased to be in a passion, sir, but—

KITE: They disobey command; they deny their being listed.

APPLETREE: Nay, serjeant, we don't downright deny it neither; that we dare not do, for fear of being shot; but we humbly conceive in a civil way, and begging your worship's pardon, that we may go home.

PLUME: That's easily known. Have either of you received any of the Queen's money?

PEARMAIN: Not a brass farthing, sir.

KITE: Sir, they have each of 'em received three-and-twenty shillings and sixpence, and 'tis now in their pockets.

PEARMAIN: Wauns, if I have a penny in my pocket but a bent sixpence, I'll be content to be listed, and shot into the bargain!

APPLETREE: And I. Look ye here, sir.

PEARMAIN: Ay, here's my stock too: nothing but the Queen's picture, that the serjeant gave me just now.

KITE: See there, a broad-piece! three-and-twenty shillings and sixpence; the t'other has the fellow on't.

PLUME: The case is plain, gentlemen; the goods are found upon you. Those pieces of gold are worth three-and-twenty and sixpence each. (*Whispers to Serjeant* KITE)

PEARMAIN: So it seems that Carolus is three-and-twenty shillings and sixpence in Latin.

APPLETREE: 'Tis the same thing in the Greek, for we are listed.

The mock beating-up takes place in the wings, with Pearmain and Appletree looking on. Pearmain's reaction: if army life gives you licence to beat people up, there must be something to it.

PEARMAIN: Flesh, but we an't, Tummas! —I desire to be carried before the Mayor, Captain.

PLUME: (*Aside to* KITE) 'Twill never do, Kite—your damned tricks will ruin me at last.—I won't lose the fellows though, if I can help it.—(*Aloud*) Well, gentlemen, there must be some trick in this: my serjeant offers here to take his oath that you are fairly listed.

APPLETREE: Why, Captain, we know that you soldiers have more liberty of conscience than other folks; but for me or neighbour Costar here to take such an oath, 'twould be a downright perjuration.

PLUME: (*To* KITE) Look'ee, you rascal! you villain! if I find that you have imposed upon these two honest fellows, I'll trample you to death, you dog! Come, how was't?

APPLETREE: Nay, then, we will speak. Your serjeant, as you say, is a rogue, begging your worships' pardon, and—

PEARMAIN: Nay, Tummas, let me speak; you know I can read.—And so, sir, he gave us those two pieces of money for pictures of the Queen, by way of a present.

PLUME: How! by way of a present! The son of a whore! I'll teach him to abuse honest fellows like you!—Scoundrel, rogue, villain! (*Beats off the* SERJEANT, *and follows*)

BOTH: O brave noble Captain! Huzza! a brave captain, faith!

PEARMAIN: Now, Tummas, Carolus is Latin for a beating. This is the bravest captain I ever saw.—Wauns, I have a month's mind to go with him!

Re-enter PLUME.

PLUME: A dog to abuse two such pretty fellows as you!—Look'ee, gentlemen, I love a pretty fellow: I come among you as an officer to list soldiers, not as a kidnapper, to steal slaves.

PEARMAIN: Mind that, Tummas.

PLUME: I desire no man to go with me but as I went myself: I went a volunteer, as you, or you, may do; for a little time carried a musket, and now I command a company.

PEARMAIN: Mind that, Tummas—A sweet gentleman!

PLUME: 'Tis true, gentlemen, I might take an advantage of you; the Queen's money was in your pockets, my serjeant was ready to take his oath you were listed; but I scorn to do a base thing. You are both of you at your liberty.

PEARMAIN: Thank you, noble captain.— Ecod, I can't find in my heart to leave him, he talks so finely.

APPLETREE: Ay, Costar, would he always hold in this mind.

PLUME: Come, my lads, one thing more I'll tell you: you're both young tight fellows, and the army is the place to make you men for ever: every man has his lot, and you have yours. What think you now of a purse full of French gold out of a monsieur's pocket, after you have dashed out his brains with the butt of your firelock, eh?

PEARMAIN: Wauns! I'll have it, Captain— give me a shilling, I'll follow you to the end of the world.

APPLETREE: Nay, dear Costar, duna; be advised.

PLUME: Here, my hero, here are two guineas for thee, as earnest of what I'll do farther for thee.

APPLETREE: Duna take it; duna, dear Costar! (Cries, and pulls back his arm)

PEARMAIN: I wull! I wull!—Wauns, my mind gives me, that I shall be a captain myself.—I take your money, sir, and now I am a gentleman.

PLUME: Give me thy hand, and now you and I will travel the world o'er, and command it wherever we tread.—(Aside to COSTAR PEARMAIN) Bring your friend with you, if you can.

PEARMAIN: Well, Tummas, must we part?

APPLETREE: No, Costar, I cannot leave thee.—Come, Captain, I'll e'en go along too; and if you have two honester simpler lads in your company than we two been, I'll say no more.

PLUME: Here, my lad.—(*Gives him money*) Now, your name?

APPLETREE: Tummas Appletree.

PLUME: And yours?

PEARMAIN: Costar Pearmain.

PLUME: Born where?

APPLETREE: Both in Herefordshire.

PLUME: Very well. Courage, my lads! Now we'll sing 'Over the hills and far away'. (*Sings*)
Courage, boys, 'tis one to ten
But we return all gentlemen;
While conquering colours we display
Over the hills and far away.

Exit Plume. Re-enter Kite.

KITE: An't you a couple of pretty fellows now! Here have you complained to the captain, I am to be turned out, and one of you will be serjeant. Which of you is to have my halberd?

BOTH: I.

KITE: So you shall—in your guts. March, you sons of whores!

Exeunt.

Kite *marches* them off—their first taste of military discipline.

Act Three

SCENE ONE

The Market-place.
Enter PLUME *and* WORTHY.

WORTHY: I cannot forbear admiring the equality of our two fortunes. We love two ladies, they met us half way, and just as we were upon the point of leaping into their arms, fortune drops into their laps, pride possesses their hearts, a maggot fills their heads, madness takes 'em by the tails; they snort, kick up their heels, and away they run.

PLUME: And leave us here to mourn upon the shore—a couple of poor melancholy monsters.—What shall we do?

WORTHY: I have a trick for mine; the letter, you know, and the fortune-teller.

PLUME: And I have a trick of mine.

WORTHY: What is't?

PLUME: I'll never think of her again.

WORTHY: No!

PLUME: No; I think myself above administering to the pride of any woman, were she worth twelve thousand a year, and I han't the vanity to believe I shall ever gain a lady worth twelve hundred. The generous good-natured Silvia in her smock I admire, but the haughty scornful Silvia, with her fortune, I despise. What, sneak out of town, and not so much as a word, a line, a compliment! 'Sdeath, how far off does she live? I'll go and break her windows.

WORTHY: Ha, ha, ha, ay, and the window-bars too, to come at her. Come, come, friend, no more of your rough military airs.

Enter KITE.

54

KITE: Captain! sir! look yonder, she's a-coming this way: 'tis the prettiest, cleanest little tit!

PLUME: Now, Worthy, to show you how much I am in love.—Here she comes; and what is that great country fellow with her?

KITE: I can't tell, sir.

Enter ROSE *and her brother* BULLOCK, ROSE *with a basket on her arm, crying chickens.*

ROSE: Buy chickens! young and tender! young and tender chickens!

Come, fair one, be kind;
You never shall find
A fellow so fit for a lover;
The world shall view
My passion for you,
But never your passion discover.

Rose's song was omitted in production.

I still will complain
Of your frowns and disdain,
Though I revel through all your charms:
The world shall declare
That I die with despair,
When I only die in your arms.

I still will adore,
And love more and more,
But, by Jove, if you chance to prove cruel,
I'll get me a miss
That freely will kiss,
Though I afterwards drink water-gruel.

PLUME: Here, you chickens!

ROSE: Who calls?

PLUME: Come hither, pretty maid.

ROSE: Will you please to buy, sir?

WORTHY: Yes, child, we'll both buy.

PLUME: Nay, Worthy, that's not fair. Market for yourself.—Come, child, I'll buy all you have.

ROSE: Then all I have is at your service. (*Curtsies*)

WORTHY: Then I must shift for myself, I find. (*Exit*)

PLUME: Let me see; young and tender you say? (*Chucks her under the chin*)

ROSE: As ever you tasted in your life, sir.

PLUME: Come, I must examine your basket to the bottom, my dear.

ROSE: Nay, for that matter, put in your hand; feel, sir; I warrant my ware as good as any in the market.

PLUME: And I'll buy it all, child, were it ten times more.

ROSE: Sir, I can furnish you.

PLUME: Come, then, we won't quarrel about the price, they're fine birds.—Pray what's your name, pretty creature?

ROSE: Rose, sir. My father is a farmer within three short mile o' the town; we keep this market; I sell chickens, eggs and butter,

and my brother Bullock there sells corn.

BULLOCK: Come, sister, hast ye, we shall be liate a whome.

All this while BULLOCK *whistles about the stage.*

PLUME: Kite! (*Tips him the wink, he returns it*) Pretty Mrs Rose—you have, let me see,—how many?

ROSE: A dozen, sir, and they are richly worth a crawn.

BULLOCK: Come Ruose, Ruose! I sold fifty stracke o' barley today in half this time; but you will higgle and higgle for a penny more than the commodity is worth.

ROSE: What's that to you, oaf? I can make as much out of a groat as you can out of fourpence, I'm sure. The gentleman bids fair, and when I meet with a chapman I know how to make the best on him.—And so, sir, I say, for a crawn-piece, the bargain's yours.

PLUME: Here's a guinea, my dear.

ROSE: I can't change your money, sir.

PLUME: Indeed, indeed, but you can: my lodging is hard by, chicken, and we'll make change there.

Goes off, she follows him.

KITE: So, sir, as I was telling you, I have seen one of these hussars eat up a ravelin for his breakfast, and afterwards pick his teeth with a palisado.

BULLOCK: Ay, you soldiers see very strange things. But pray, sir, what is a ravelin?

KITE: Why, 'tis like a modern minced pie, but the crust is confounded hard, and the plums are somewhat hard of digestion.

BULLOCK: Then your palisado, pray what may he be?—Come, Ruose, pray ha' done.

KITE: Your palisado is a pretty sort of bodkin, about the thickness of my leg.

BULLOCK: (*Aside*) That's a fib, I believe.—

(*Aloud*) Eh! where's Ruose? Ruose! Ruose! 'sflesh, where's Ruose gone?

KITE: She's gone with the captain.

BULLOCK: If the captain should press Ruose I should be ruined! Which way went she? Oh, the devil take your rablins and your palisaders!

Exit.

KITE: You shall be better acquainted with them, honest Bullock, or I shall miss of my aim.

Re-enter WORTHY.

WORTHY: Why, thou art the most useful fellow in nature to your captain; admirable in your way, I find.

KITE: Yes, sir, I understand my business, I will say it.—You must know, sir, I was born a gipsy, and bred among that crew till I was ten year old. There I learnt canting and lying. I was bought from my mother, Cleopatra, by a certain nobleman for three pistoles; who, liking my beauty, made me his page; there I learnt impudence and pimping. I was turned off for wearing my lord's linen, and drinking my lady's ratafia, and then turned bailiff's follower: there I learnt bullying and swearing. I at last got into the army, and there I learnt whoring and drinking: so that if your worship pleases to cast up the whole sum, viz., canting, lying, impudence, pimping, bullying, swearing, whoring, drinking, and a halberd, you will find the sum total will amount to a recruiting sergeant.

WORTHY: And pray what induced you to turn soldier?

KITE: Hunger and ambition. The fears of starving, the hopes of a truncheon, led me along to a gentleman with a fair tongue and fair periwig, who loaded me with promises; but, egad, it was the lightest load that ever I felt in my life. He promised to advance me, and indeed he did—to a garret in Savoy barracks. I asked him why he put me in prison; he called me lying dog, and said I was in garrison; and indeed 'tis a garrison that may hold out till doomsday before I should desire to take it again. But here comes Justice Balance.

Enter BALANCE *and* BULLOCK.

BALANCE: Here, you sergeant, where's your captain? Here's a poor foolish fellow comes clamouring to me with a complaint that your captain has pressed his sister.— Do you know anything of this matter, Worthy?

WORTHY: Ha, ha, ha! I know his sister is gone with Plume to his lodging, to sell him some chickens.

BALANCE: Is that all? The fellow's a fool.

BULLOCK: I know that, an't please you; but if your worship pleases to grant me a warrant to bring her before you, for fear o' th' worst.

BALANCE: Thou'rt mad, fellow; thy sister's safe enough.

KITE: (*Aside*) I hope so too.

WORTHY: Hast thou no more sense, fellow, than to believe that the captain can press women?

BULLOCK: I know not whether they press them, or what they do with them, but, I am sure, they carry as many women as men with them out of the country.

BALANCE: But how came you not to go along with your sister?

BULLOCK: Luord, sir, I thought no more of her going than I do of the day I shall die; but this gentleman here, not suspecting any hurt neither, I believe,—(*To* KITE) You thought no harm, friend, did ye?

KITE: Lackaday, sir, not I! (*Aside*) Only that I believe I shall marry her tomorrow.

BALANCE: I begin to smell powder.— Well, friend, but what did that gentleman with you?

BULLOCK: He entertained me with a fine story of a sea fight between the Hungarians, I think it was, and the wild Irish; and while we were in the heat of the battle—the Captain carried off the baggage.

BALANCE: Sergeant, go along with this fellow to your Captain, give him my humble service, and desire him to discharge the wench, though he has listed her.

BULLOCK: Ay, and if he ben't free for that, he shall have another man in her place.

KITE: Come, honest friend.—(*Aside*) You shall go to my quarters instead of the Captain's.

Exit with BULLOCK.

BALANCE: We must get this mad captain his complement of men, and send him a-packing, else he'll overrun the country.

WORTHY: You see, sir, how little he values your daughter's disdain.

BALANCE: I like him the better; I was just such another fellow at his age. I never set my heart upon any woman so much as to make myself uneasy at the disappointment; but what was very surprising both to myself and friends, I changed o' th' sudden from the most fickle lover to the most constant husband in the world. But how goes

Brazen is glimpsed crossing the stage at rear. He disappears R., only to make another 'subliminal' entrance and exit, crossing R. to L., before re-entering L. and spotting Worthy. This triple entrance helps to establish the man's total vagueness and inability to concentrate on anything for more than a few moments.

your affair with Melinda?

WORTHY: Very slowly. Cupid had formerly wings, but I think, in this age, he goes upon crutches; or, I fancy Venus has been dallying with her cripple Vulcan when my amour commenced, which has made it go on so lamely. My mistress has got a captain too, but such a captain! As I live, yonder he comes?

BALANCE: Who? That bluff fellow in the sash! I don't know him.

WORTHY: But I engage he knows you, and everybody, at first sight: his impudence were a prodigy were not his ignorance proportionable. He has the most universal acquaintance of any man living; for he won't be alone, and nobody will keep him company twice. Then he's a Caesar among the women, Veni, vidi, vici, that's all: if he has but talked with the maid, he swears he has lain with the mistress. But the most surprising part of his character is his memory, which is the most prodigious and the most trifling in the world.

BALANCE: I have met with such men; and I take this good-for-nothing memory to proceed from a certain contexture of the brain, which is purely adapted to impertinencies, and there they lodge secure, the owner having no thoughts of his own to disturb them. I have known a man as perfect as a chronologer as to the day and year of the most important transactions, but be altogether ignorant of the causes or consequences of any one thing of moment. I have known another acquire so much by travel as to tell you the names of most places in Europe, with their distances of miles, leagues, or hours, as punctually as a postboy; but for anything else, as ignorant as the horse that carries the mail.

WORTHY: This is your man, sir: add but the traveller's privilege of lying; and even that he abuses. This is the picture, behold the life.

Enter BRAZEN.

BRAZEN: Mr Worthy, I am your servant, and so forth.—Hark'ee, my dear.

WORTHY: Whispering, sir, before company is not manners, and when nobody's by 'tis foolish.

BRAZEN: Company! Mort de ma vie! I beg the gentleman's pardon; who is he?

WORTHY: Ask him.

BRAZEN: So I will.—My dear, I am your servant, and so forth—your name, my dear?

BALANCE: Very laconic, sir!

BRAZEN: Laconic! a very good name, truly; I have known several of the Laconics abroad.—Poor Jack Laconic! He was killed at the battle of Landen. I remember that he had a blue ribbon in his hat that very day, and after he fell we found a piece of neat's tongue in his pocket.

BALANCE: Pray, sir, did the French attack us, or we them, at Landen?

BRAZEN: The French attack us! Oons, sir, are you a Jacobite?

BALANCE: Why that question?

BRAZEN: Because none but a Jacobite could think that the French durst attack us. No, sir, we attacked them on the—I have reason to remember the time, for I had two-and-twenty horses killed under me that day.

WORTHY: Then, sir, you must have rid mighty hard.

BALANCE: Or perhaps, sir, like my countryman, you rid upon half-a-dozen horses at once.

BRAZEN: What do you mean, gentlemen? I tell you they were killed, all torn to pieces by cannon-shot, except six I staked to death upon the enemy's chevaux-de-frise.

BALANCE: Noble Captain, may I crave your name?

BRAZEN: Brazen, at your service.

BALANCE: Oh, Brazen, a very good name;

I have known several of the Brazens abroad.

WORTHY: Do you know Captain Plume, sir?

BRAZEN: Is he anything related to Frank Plume of Northamptonshire?—Honest Frank! many, many a dry bottle have we cracked hand to fist. You must have known his brother Charles that was concerned in the India Company; he married the daughter of old Tonguepad, the Master in Chancery, a very pretty woman, only squinted a little. She died in childbed of her first child, but the child survived; 'twas a daughter, but whether 'twas called Margaret or Margery, upon my soul, I can't remember.—(*looking on his watch*) But, gentlemen, I must meet a lady, a twenty thousand pounder, presently, upon the walk by the water.—Worthy, your servant.—Laconic, yours. (*Exit*)

BALANCE: If you can have so mean an opinion of Melinda as to be jealous of this fellow, I think she ought to give you cause to be so.

WORTHY: I don't think she encourages him so much for gaining herself a lover, as to set me up a rival. Were there any credit to be given to his words, I should believe Melinda had made him this assignation. I must go see; sir, you'll pardon me.

BALANCE: Ay, ay, sir, you're a man of business.—

Exit MR WORTHY.

But what have we got here?

Re-enter ROSE, *singing*.

ROSE: And I shall be a lady, a captain's lady, and ride single upon a white horse with a star, upon a velvet side-saddle; and I shall go to London, and see the tombs, and the lions, and the Queen.—Sir, an please your worship, I have often seen your worship ride through our grounds a-hunt-

ing, begging your worship's pardon—pray what may this lace be worth a yard? (*Showing some lace*)

BALANCE: Right Mechlin, by this light! Where did you get this lace, child?

ROSE: No matter for that, sir; I come honestly by it.

BALANCE: I question it much.

ROSE: And see here, sir, a fine Turkey-shell snuff-box and fine mangeree, see here.—(*Takes snuff affectedly*) The captain learned me how to take it with an air.

BALANCE: Oho! the captain! Now the murder's out. And so the captain taught you to take it with an air?

ROSE: Yes, and give it with an air too.— Will your worship please to taste my snuff. (*Offers the box affectedly*)

BALANCE: You are a very apt scholar, pretty maid. And pray, what did you give the captain for these fine things?

ROSE: He's to have my brother for a soldier, and two or three sweethearts that I have in the country, they shall all go with the captain. Oh, he's the finest man, and

the humblest withal! Would you believe it, sir, he carried me up with him to his own chamber, with as much familiarity as if I had been the best lady in the land!

BALANCE: Oh! he's a mighty familiar gentleman, as can be.

Re-enter PLUME, *singing.*

PLUME: But it is not so
        With those that go,
        Through frost and snow.
        Most àpropos,
        My maid with the milking-pail.
        (*Takes hold of* ROSE)

(*Aside*) How, the Justice! then I'm arraigned, condemned, and executed.

BALANCE: Oh, my noble Captain!

ROSE: And my noble Captain too, sir.

PLUME: (*Aside to* ROSE) 'Sdeath, child! are you mad? (*Aloud*) Mr Balance, I am so full of business about my recruits, that I han't a moment's time to—I have just now three or four people to—

BALANCE: Nay, Captain, I must speak to you—

ROSE: And so must I too, Captain.

PLUME: Any other time, sir—I cannot for my life, sir—

BALANCE: Pray, sir—

PLUME: Twenty thousand things—I would —but now, sir, pray—devil take me—I cannot—I must—(*Breaks away*)

BALANCE: Nay, I'll follow you. (*Exit*)

ROSE: And I too. (*Exit*)

Scene-change from town to countryside —René Allio's second transformation effect.

Act Three

SCENE TWO

The walk by the Severn side.
Enter MELINDA *and* LUCY.

MELINDA: And pray was it a ring, or buckle, or pendants, or knots? Or in what shape was the almighty gold transformed that has bribed you so in Mr Worthy's favour?

LUCY: Indeed, madam, the last bribe I had was from Captain Brazen, and that only a small piece of Flanders edging for pinners.

MELINDA: Ay, Flanders lace is as constant a present from officers to their women as something else is from their women to them. They every year bring over a cargo of lace, to cheat the Queen of her duty, and her subjects of their honesty.

LUCY: They only barter one sort of prohibited goods for another, madam.

MELINDA: Has any of 'em been bartering with you, Mrs Pert, that you talk so like a trader?

LUCY: Madam, you talk as peevishly to me as if it were my fault; the crime is none of mine, though I pretend to excuse it: though he should not see you this week, can I help it? But as I was saying, madam—his friend, Captain Plume, has so taken him up these two days.

MELINDA: Psha! Would his friend, the captain, were tied upon his back! I warrant he has never been sober since that confounded captain came to town. The devil take all officers, I say! They do the nation more harm by debauching us at home than they do good by defending us abroad. No sooner a captain comes to town but all the young fellows flock about him, and we can't keep

a man to ourselves.

LUCY: One would imagine, madam, by your concern for Worthy's absence, that you should use him better when he's with you.

MELINDA: Who told you, pray, that I was concerned for his absence? I'm only vexed that I've had nothing said to me these two days. One may like the love and despise the lover, I hope; as one may love the treason and hate the traitor.— Oh, here comes the other captain, and a rogue that has the confidence to make love to me; but, indeed, I don't wonder at that, when he has the assurance to fancy himself a fine gentleman.

LUCY: (*Aside*) If he should speak o' th' assignation I should be ruined.

Enter BRAZEN.

BRAZEN: (*Aside*) True to the touch, faith!— (*Aloud*) Madam, I am your humble servant, and all that, madam.—A fine river, this same Severn.—Do you love fishing, madam?

MELINDA: 'Tis a pretty, melancholy amusement for lovers.

BRAZEN: I'll go buy hooks and lines presently; for you must know, madam, that I have served in Flanders against the French, in Hungary against the Turks, and in Tangier against the Moors, and I was never so much in love before; and split me, madam, in all the campaigns I ever made, I have not seen so fine a woman as your ladyship.

MELINDA: And from all the men I ever saw I never had so fine a compliment; but you soldiers are the best bred men, that we must allow.

BRAZEN: Some of us, madam.—But there are brutes among us too, very sad brutes; for my own part, I have always had the good luck to prove agreeable.—I have had very considerable offers, madam—I might have married a German princess, worth fifty thousand crowns a year, but her stove dis-

Brazen slaps her jovially on the bottom.

Brazen takes Melinda's hand, and instead of kissing it, puts out his tongue and *licks* it.

gusted me.—The daughter of a Turkish bashaw fell in love with me too, when I was prisoner among the Infidels; she offered to rob her father of his treasure, and make her escape with me; but I don't know how, my time was not come. Hanging and marriage, you know, go by destiny; Fate has reserved me for a Shropshire lady with twenty thousand pounds.—Do you know any such person, madam?

MELINDA: (*Aside*) Extravagant coxcomb!—(*Aloud*) To be sure, a great many ladies of that fortune would be proud of the name of Mrs Brazen.

BRAZEN: Nay, for that matter, madam, there are women of very good quality of the name of Brazen.

Enter WORTHY.

MELINDA: (*Aside*) Oh, are you there, gentlemen? (*Aloud*) Come, Captain, we'll walk this way; give me your hand.

BRAZEN: My hand, heart's blood, and guts are at your service.—Mr Worthy, your servant, my dear.

Exit, leading MELINDA, LUCY *following.*

WORTHY: Death and fire, this is not to be borne!

Enter Captain PLUME.

PLUME: No more it is, faith.

WORTHY: What?

PLUME: The March beer at the Raven. I have been doubly serving the Queen—raising men, and raising the excise. Recruiting and elections are rare friends to the excise.

WORTHY: You an't drunk?

PLUME: No, no, whimsical only: I could be mighty foolish and fancy myself mighty witty. Reason still keeps its throne, but it nods a little, that's all.

WORTHY: Then you're just fit for a frolic.

PLUME: As fit as close pinners for a punk in the pit.

WORTHY: There's your play, then—recover me that vessel from that Tangerine.

PLUME: She's well rigged, but how is she manned?

WORTHY: By Captain Brazen, that I told you of to-day. She is called the Melinda, a first-rater, I can assure you; she sheered off with him just now, on purpose to affront me; but, according to your advice, I would take no notice, because I would seem to be above a concern for her behaviour.—But have a care of a quarrel.

PLUME: No, no, I never quarrel with anything in my cups, but an oyster wench, or a cookmaid; and if they ben't civil, I knock 'em down. But heark'ee, my friend, I'll make love, and I must make love. I tell you what, I'll make love like a platoon.

WORTHY: Platoon, how's that?

PLUME: I'll kneel, stoop, and stand, faith; most ladies are gained by platooning.

WORTHY: Here they come; I must leave you. (*Exit*)

PLUME: Soh! Now must I look as sober and demure as a whore at a christening.

Re-enter BRAZEN *and* MELINDA.

BRAZEN: Who's that, madam?

MELINDA: A brother officer of yours, I suppose, sir.

BRAZEN: Ay!—(*To* PLUME) My dear!

PLUME: My dear!

Run and embrace: they kiss on the lips.

BRAZEN: My dear boy, how is't? Your name, my dear? If I be not mistaken, I have seen your face.

PLUME: I never saw yours in my life, my dear.—But there's a face well known as the sun's, that shines on all and is by all adored.

BRAZEN: Have you any pretensions, sir?

PLUME: Pretensions!

BRAZEN: That is, sir, have you ever

At 'stand', Plume raises his stick and squints along it like a rifle.

served abroad?

PLUME: I have served at home, sir, for ages served this cruel fair—and that will serve the turn, sir.

MELINDA: (*Aside*) So, between the fool and the rake I shall bring a fine spot of work upon my hands!—I see Worthy yonder—I could be content to be friends with him, would he come this way.

BRAZEN: Will you fight for the lady, sir?

PLUME: No, sir, but I'll have her not withstanding.

Thou peerless princess of Salopian plains,
Envied by nymphs, and worshipp'd by the swains!

BRAZEN: Oons, sir, not fight for her!

PLUME: Prithee be quiet—I shall be out—

Behold how humbly does the Severn glide
To greet thee, princess of the Severn side!

BRAZEN: Don't mind him, madam.—If he were not so well dressed, I should take him for a poet.—But I'll show the difference presently.—Come, madam, we'll place you between us; and now the longest sword carried her.

Draws, MELINDA *shrieks.*
Re-enter WORTHY.

MELINDA: Oh! Mr Worthy! save me from these madmen.

Exit with WORTHY.

PLUME: Ha, ha, ha! why don't you follow, sir, and fight the bold ravisher?

BRAZEN: No, sir, you are my man.

PLUME: I don't like the wages, and I won't be your man.

BRAZEN: Then you're not worth my sword.

PLUME: No! Pray what did it cost?

BRAZEN: It cost me twenty pistoles in France, and my enemies thousands of lives in Flanders.

PLUME: Then they had a dear bargain.

As Wilful, Silvia wears a moustache: an idea borrowed from the Berliner Ensemble production of 'Drums and Trumpets'.

Enter SILVIA, *in man's apparel.*

SILVIA: Save ye, save ye, gentlemen!

BRAZEN: My dear, I'm yours.

PLUME: Do you know the gentleman?

BRAZEN: No, but I will presently.—(*To* SILVIA) Your name, my dear?

SILVIA: Wilful; Jack Wilful, at your service.

BRAZEN: What, the Kentish Wilfuls, or those of Staffordshire?

SILVIA: Both, sir, both; I'm related to all the Wilfuls in Europe, and I'm head of the family at present.

PLUME: Do you live in this country, sir?

SILVIA: Yes, sir, I live where I stand; I have neither home, house, nor habitation, beyond this spot of ground.

BRAZEN: What are you, sir?

SILVIA: A rake.

PLUME: In the army, I presume.

SILVIA: No, but I intend to list immediately. —Look'ee, gentlemen, he that bids me fairest shall have me.

BRAZEN: Sir, I'll prefer you, I'll make you a corporal this minute.

PLUME: Corporal! I'll make you my companion; you shall eat with me.

BRAZEN: You shall drink with me.

PLUME: You shall lie with me, you young rogue. (*Kisses her*)

BRAZEN: You shall receive your pay, and do no duty.

SILVIA: Then you must make me a field officer.

PLUME: Pho! pho! I'll do more than all this; I'll make you a corporal, and give you a brevet for serjeant.

BRAZEN: Can you read and write, sir?

SILVIA: Yes.

BRAZEN: Then your business is done—I'll

make you chaplain to the regiment.

SILVIA: Your promises are so equal, that I'm at a loss to choose. There is one Plume, that I hear much commended, in town; pray, which of you is Captain Plume?

PLUME: I am Captain Plume.

BRAZEN: No, no, I am Captain Plume.

SILVIA: Heyday!

PLUME: Captain Plume! I'm your servant, my dear.

BRAZEN: Captain Brazen! I am yours.— (*Aside*) The fellow dare not fight.

Enter KITE.

KITE: (*Goes to whisper to* PLUME) Sir, if you please—

PLUME: No, no, there's your captain—Captain Plume, your serjeant here has got so drunk, he mistakes me for you.

BRAZEN: He's an incorrigible sot!—(*To* SILVIA) Here, my Hector of Holborn, forty shillings for you.

PLUME: I forbid the banns.—Look'ee, friend, you shall list with Captain Brazen.

SILVIA: I will see Captain Brazen hanged first! I will list with Captain Plume. I am a freeborn Englishman, and will be a slave my own way.—(*To* BRAZEN) Look'ee sir, will you stand by me?

BRAZEN: I warrant you, my lad.

SILVIA: (*To* PLUME) Then I will tell you, Captain Brazen, that you are an ignorant, pretending, impudent coxcomb.

BRAZEN: Ay, ay, a sad dog.

SILVIA: A very sad dog.—Give me the money, noble Captain Plume.

PLUME: Then you won't list with Captain Brazen?

SILVIA: I won't.

BRAZEN: Never mind him, child, I'll end the dispute presently.—Heark'ee my dear.

Takes PLUME *to one side of the stage, and*

75

entertains him in dumb show.

KITE: Sir, he in the plain coat is Captain Plume, I am his serjeant, and will take my oath on't.

SILVIA: What! are you Serjeant Kite?

KITE: At your service.

SILVIA: Then I would not take your oath for a farthing.

KITE: A very understanding youth of his age!—Pray, sir, let me look you full in the face.

SILVIA: Well, sir, what have you to say to my face.

KITE: The very image and superscription of my brother; two bullets of the same caliver were never so like: sure it must be Charles, Charles!

SILVIA: What d'ye mean by Charles?

KITE: The voice too, only a little variation in Effa-ut flat. My dear brother, for I must call you so, if you should have the fortune to enter into the most noble society of the sword, I bespeak you for a comrade.

SILVIA: No, sir, I'll be your captain's comrade, if anybodys'.

KITE: Ambition there again! 'Tis a noble passion for a soldier; by that I gained this glorious halberd. Ambition! I see a commission in his face already. Pray, noble captain, give me leave to salute you. (*Offers to kiss her*)

SILVIA: What, men kiss one another!

KITE: We officers do: 'tis our way; we live together like man and wife, always either kissing or fighting.—But I see a storm a-coming.

SILVIA: Now, serjeant, I shall see who is your captain by your knocking down the t'other.

KITE: My captain scorns assistance, sir.

BRAZEN: How dare you contend for anything, and not dare to draw your sword?

Since Kite does not suspect Silvia's identity, only one interpretation of this exchange is possible: that for soldiers on active service, as for the sailor in *Fanny Hill*, it is often a case of 'any port in a storm'. The Brazen-Plume embraces, on the other hand, are merely salutations, *sans* sex.

Kite chases Silvia offstage.

But you're a young fellow, and have not been much abroad; I excuse that, but prithee resign the man, prithee do; you're a very honest fellow.

PLUME: You lie; and you are a son of a whore. (*Draws and makes up to* BRAZEN)

BRAZEN: Hold! Hold! did not you refuse to fight? (*Retiring*)

PLUME: For the lady, yes—but for a man I'll fight knee deep; so you lie again.

(PLUME *and* BRAZEN *fight a traverse or two about the stage*)

BRAZEN: Hold! where's the man?

PLUME: Gone.

BRAZEN: Then what do you fight for? (*Puts up*) Now let's embrace, my dear.

PLUME: With all my heart, my dear. (*Putting up*) I suppose Kite has listed him by this time.

They embrace.

A switch: Silvia dashes across the stage in hot pursuit of Kite.

As they embrace, Kite reappears behind them carrying Silvia off perched on his shoulders.

BRAZEN: You are a brave fellow. I always fight with a man before I make him my friend; and if once I find he will fight, I never quarrel with him afterwards. And now I'll tell you a secret, my dear friend; that lady we frighted out of the walk just now I found in bed this morning—so beautiful, so inviting!—I presently locked the door—but I am a man of honour.—But I believe I shall marry her nevertheless; her twenty thousand pound, you know, will be a pretty convenience.—I had an assignation with her here, but your coming spoiled my sport. Curse you, my dear, but don't do so again.

PLUME: No, no, my dear, men are my business at present.

Exeunt.

Act Four

SCENE ONE

The walk by the Severn.
Enter ROSE *and* BULLOCK, *meeting.*

ROSE: Where have you been, you great booby? You're always out o' the way in the time of preferment.

BULLOCK: Preferment! who should prefer me?

ROSE: I would prefer you! Who should prefer a man but a woman? Come, throw away that great club, hold up your head, cock your hat, and look big.

BULLOCK: Ah, Ruose, Ruose, I fear somebody will look big sooner than folk think of! This genteel breeding never comes into the country without a train of followers.— Here has been Cartwheel, your sweetheart; what will become o' him?

ROSE: Look'ee, I'm a great woman, and will provide for my relations. I told the captain how finely he could play upon the tabor and pipe, so he has set him down for drum-major.

BULLOCK: Nay, sister, why did not you keep that place for me! You know I always loved to be a-drumming, if it were but on a table or on a quart pot.

Enter SILVIA.

SILVIA: Had I but a commission in my pocket, I fancy my breeches would become me as well as any ranting fellow of 'em all; for I take a bold step, a rakish toss, a smart cock, and an impudent air, to be the principal ingredients in the composition of a captain.—What's here: Rose! my nurse's daughter!—I'll go and practise.—Come, child, kiss me at once.—(*Kisses* ROSE) And her brother too!—(*To* BULLOCK) Well, honest dung-fork, do you know the difference between a horse-cart and a cart-horse, eh?

BULLOCK: I presume that your worship is a captain by your clothes and your courage.

SILVIA: Suppose I were, would you be contented to list, friend?

ROSE: No, no, though your worship be a handsome man, there be others as fine as you; my brother is engaged to Captain Plume.

SILVIA: Plume! do you know Captain Plume?

Rose in this passage is not coquettish— just a simple clod putting her foot in it.

ROSE: Yes, I do, and he knows me. He took the very ribbons out of his shirt-sleeves, and put 'em into my shoes. See there!—I can assure you that I can do anything with the captain.

BULLOCK: That is, in a modest way, sir.— Have a care what you say, Ruose, don't shame your parentage.

ROSE: Nay, for that matter, I am not so simple as to say that I can do anything with the captain but what I may do with anybody else.

SILVIA: So!—And pray what do you expect from this captain, child?

ROSE: I expect, sir—I expect—but he ordered me to tell nobody.—But suppose that he should promise to marry me?

SILVIA: You should have a care, my dear, men will promise anything beforehand.

ROSE: I know that, but he promised to marry me afterwards.

BULLOCK: Wauns, Ruose, what have you said?

SILVIA: Afterwards! after what?

ROSE: After I had sold him my chickens.— I hope there's no harm in that.

Enter PLUME.

PLUME: What, Mr Wilful, so close with my market woman!

SILVIA: (*Aside*) I'll try if he loves her.—(*Aloud*) Close, sir! ay, and closer yet, sir.—Come, my pretty maid, you and I will withdraw a little—

PLUME: No, no, friend, I han't done with her yet.

SILVIA: Nor have I begun with her, so I have as good right as you have.

PLUME: Thou are a bloody impudent fellow.

SILVIA: Sir, I would qualify myself for the service.

PLUME: Hast thou really a mind to the service?

Silvia and Plume engage in a tug-of-war with Rose in the middle.

SILVIA: Yes, sir: so let her go.

ROSE: Pray, gentlemen, don't be so violent.

PLUME: Come, leave it to the girl's own choice.—Will you belong to me or to that gentleman?

ROSE: Let me consider: you are both very handsome.

PLUME: (*Aside*) Now the natural unconstancy of her sex begins to work.

ROSE: Pray, sir, what will you give me?

BULLOCK: Don't be angry, sir, that my sister should be mercenary, for she's but young.

SILVIA: Give thee, child! I'll set thee above scandal; you shall have a coach with six before and six behind, an equipage to make vice fashionable, and put virtue out of countenance.

PLUME: Pho! that's easily done.—I'll do more for thee, child; I'll buy you a furbelow scarf, and give you a ticket to see a play.

BULLOCK: A play! Wauns, Ruose, take the ticket, and let's see the show.

SILVIA: Look'ee, Captain, if you won't resign, I'll go list with Captain Brazen this minute.

PLUME: Will you list with me if I give up my title?

SILVIA: I will.

PLUME: Take her: I'll change a woman for a man at any time.

ROSE: I have heard before, indeed, that you captains used to sell your men.

BULLOCK: Pray, Captain, do not send Ruose to the West Indies. (*Cries*)

PLUME: Ha, ha, ha! West Indies!—No, no, my honest lad, give me thy hand; nor you nor she shall move a step further than I do. —This gentleman is one of us, and will be kind to you, Mrs Rose.

ROSE: But will you be so kind to me, sir, as the captain would?

SILVIA: I can't be altogether so kind to you, my circumstances are not so good as the captain's; but I'll take care of you, upon my word.

PLUME: Ay, ay, we'll all take care of her; she shall live like a princess, and her brother here shall be—What would you be?

BULLOCK: Oh, sir! if you had not promised the place of drum-major—

PLUME: Ay, that is promised. But what think you of barrack-master? You are a person of understanding, and barrack-master you shall be.—But what's become of this same Cartwheel you told me of, my dear?

ROSE: We'll go fetch him.—Come, brother barrack-master.—We shall find you at home, noble Captain?

PLUME: Yes, yes.—

Exeunt ROSE *and* BULLOCK.

And now, sir, here are your forty shillings.

SILVIA: Captain Plume, I despise your listing money; if I do serve, 'tis purely for love —of that wench, I mean. For you must know that, among my other sallies, I have spent the best part of my fortune in search of a maid, and could never find one hitherto: so you may be assured I'd not sell my freedom under a less purchase than I did my estate. So, before I list, I must be certified that this girl is a virgin.

PLUME: Mr Wilful, I can't tell you how you can be certified in that point till you try; but upon my honour, she may be a vestal for aught that I know to the contrary. I gained

Insisting on a virgin is of course evidence of lubricity, not primness. Silvia is trying to pass herself off as a thoroughly jaded rake.

her heart, indeed, by some trifling presents and promises, and, knowing that the best security for a woman's soul is her body, I would have made myself master of that too, had not the jealousy of my impertinent landlady interposed.

SILVIA: So you only want an opportunity for accomplishing your designs upon her?

PLUME: Not at all; I have already gained my ends, which were only the drawing in one or two of her followers. The women, you know, are the loadstones everywhere; gain the wives, and you are caressed by the husbands; please the mistresses, and you are valued by the gallants; secure an interest with the finest women at the court, and you procure the favour of the greatest men: so, kiss the prettiest country wenches, and you are sure of listing the lustiest fellows. Some people may call this artifice, but I term it stratagem, since it is so main a part of the service. Besides, the fatigue of recruiting is so intolerable, that unless we could make ourselves some pleasure amidst the pain, no mortal man would be able to bear it.

SILVIA: Well, sir, I am satisfied as to the point in debate. But now let me beg you to lay aside your recruiting airs, put on the man of honour, and tell me plainly what usage I must expect when I am under your command?

PLUME: You must know, in the first place, then, that I hate to have gentlemen in my company; for they are always troublesome and expensive, sometimes dangerous; and 'tis a constant maxim amongst us, that those who know the least obey the best. Notwithstanding all this, I find something so agreeable about you, that engages me to court your company; and I can't tell how it is, but I should be uneasy to see you under the command of anybody else. Your usage will chiefly depend upon your behaviour; only this you must expect, that if you commit a small fault I will excuse it, if

'The idea that the army should be a microcosm of the nation, or representative of it in any true sense, would have seemed to most contemporaries ridiculous or even shocking. It was generally agreed that it should be raised from the social groups of least economic value. "It would undoubtedly be desirable," wrote the Comte de Saint-Germain, perhaps the greatest French war minister of the century, "if we could create an army of dependable and specially-selected men of the best type. But . . . as things are, the army must inevitably consist of the scum

86

of the people and of all those for whom society has no use . . ." '—from *Europe in the Eighteenth Century* by M. S. Anderson.

This is an honest confession on Plume's part—and he makes it to Wilful, the professed rake, with some embarrassment.

a great one I'll discharge you; for something tells me I shall not be able to punish you.

SILVIA: And something tells me, that if you do discharge me, 'twill be the greatest punishment you can inflict; for were we this moment to go upon the greatest dangers in your profession, they would be less terrible to me than to stay behind you.—And now your hand, this lists me—and now you are my Captain.

PLUME: (*Kissing her*) Your friend.—(*Aside*) 'Sdeath! there's something in this fellow that charms me.

SILVIA: One favour I must beg. This affair will make some noise, and I have some friends that would censure my conduct if I threw myself into the circumstance of a private sentinel of my own head: I must therefore take care to be impressed by the Act of Parliament; you shall leave that to me.

PLUME: What you please as to that.—Will you lodge at my quarters in the meantime? you shall have part of my bed.

SILVIA: O fy! lie with a common soldier! Would not you rather lie with a common woman?

PLUME: No, faith, I'm not that rake that the world imagines: I have got an air of freedom, which people mistake for lewdness in me, as they mistake formality in others for religion. The world is all a cheat; only I take mine, which is undesigned, to be more excusable than theirs, which is hypocritical. I hurt nobody but myself, and they abuse all mankind. Will you lie with me?

SILVIA: No, no, Captain, you forget Rose; she's to be my bedfellow, you know.

PLUME: I had forgot; pray be kind to her.

Exeunt severally.

Act Four

SCENE TWO

Enter MELINDA *and* LUCY.

MELINDA: (*Aside*) 'Tis the greatest misfortune in nature for a woman to want a confidant! We are so weak that we can do nothing without assistance, and then a secret racks us worse than the colic. I am at this minute so sick of a secret, that I'm ready to faint away.—(*Aloud*) Help me, Lucy!

LUCY: Bless me, madam! what's the matter?

MELINDA: Vapours only, I begin to recover.—(*Aside*) If Silvia were in town, I could heartily forgive her faults for the ease of discovering my own.

LUCY: You're thoughtful, madam; am not I worthy to know the cause?

MELINDA: You are a servant, and a secret would make you saucy.

LUCY: Not unless you should find fault without a cause, madam.

MELINDA: Cause or not cause, I must not lose the pleasure of chiding when I please; women must discharge their vapours somewhere, and before we get husbands our servants must expect to bear with 'em.

LUCY: Then, madam, you had better raise me to a degree above a servant. You know my family, and that five hundred pounds would set me upon the foot of a gentlewoman, and make me worthy the confidence of any lady in the land. Besides, madam, 'twill extremely encourage me in the great design I now have in hand.

MELINDA: I don't find that your design can

be of any great advantage to you. 'Twill please me, indeed, in the humour I have of being revenged on the fool for his vanity of making love to me, so I don't much care if I do promise you five hundred pounds upon my day of marriage.

LUCY: That is the way, madam, to make me diligent in the vocation of a confidant, which I think is generally to bring people together.

MELINDA: O Lucy! I can hold my secret no longer. You must know, that hearing of the famous fortune-teller in town, I went disguised to satisfy a curiosity, which has cost me dear. That fellow is certainly the devil, or one of his bosom favourites; he has told me the most surprising things of my past life—

LUCY: Things past, madam, can hardly be reckoned surprising, because we know them already. Did he tell you anything surprising that was to come?

MELINDA: One thing very surprising; he said I should die a maid!

LUCY: Die a maid! come into the world for nothing! Dear madam, if you should believe him, it might come to pass, for the bare thought on't might kill one in four-and-twenty hours.—And did you ask him any questions about me?

MELINDA: You! Why, I passed for you.

LUCY: So, 'tis I that am to die a maid!—But the devil was a liar from the beginning; he can't make me die a maid.—(*Aside*) I have put it out of his power already.

MELINDA: I do but jest. I would have passed for you, and called myself Lucy; but he presently told me my name, my quality, my fortune, and gave me the whole history of my life. He told me of a lover I had in this country, and described Worthy exactly, but in nothing so well as in his present indifference. I fled to him for refuge here to-day; he never so much as encouraged me in my fright, but coldly told me that he was sorry

Worthy stoops to pick up his snuff-box: Brazen replaces him at Melinda's side and receives the slap intended for Worthy.

for the accident, because it might give the town cause to censure my conduct; exused his not waiting on me home, made me a careless bow, and walked off. 'Sdeath! I could have stabbed him, or myself, 'twas the same thing.—Yonder he comes—I will so use him!

LUCY: Don't exasperate him; consider what the fortune-teller told you. Men are scarce, and, as times go, it is not impossible for a woman to die a maid.

MELINDA: No matter.

Enter WORTHY.

WORTHY: (*Aside*) I find she's warmed; I must strike while the iron is hot.—(*Aloud*) You have a great deal of courage, madam, to venture into the walks where you were so lately frightened.

MELINDA: And you have a quantity of impudence to appear before me, that you have so lately affronted.

WORTHY: I had no design to affront you, nor appear before you either, madam: I left you here, because I had business in another place, and came hither, thinking to meet another person.

MELINDA: Since you find yourself disappointed, I hope you'll withdraw to another part of the walk.

WORTHY: The walk is as free for me as you, madam, and broad enough for us both.

They walk by one another, he with his hat cocked, she fretting and tearing her fan.

Will you please to take snuff, madam?

Offers her his box, she strikes it out of his hand; while he is gathering it up, enter BRAZEN

BRAZEN: What, here before me, my dear! (*Takes MELINDA round the waist*)

MELINDA: What means this insolence? (*She cuffs him*)

LUCY: (*To BRAZEN*) Are you mad? don't

you see Mr Worthy?

BRAZEN: No, no, I'm struck blind.—Worthy! odso! well turned!—My mistress has wit at her fingers' ends.—Madam, I ask your pardon, 'tis our way abroad.—Mr Worthy, you are the happy man.

WORTHY: I don't envy your happiness very much, if the lady can afford no other sort of favours but what she has bestowed upon you.

MELINDA: I am sorry the favour miscarried, for it was designed for you, Mr Worthy; and be assured, 'tis the last and only favour you must expect at my hands.—Captain, I ask your pardon.

BRAZEN: I grant it.

Exeunt MELINDA *and* LUCY.

You see, Mr Worthy, 'twas only a random shot; it might have taken off your head as well as mine. Courage, my dear! 'tis the fortune of war.—But the enemy has thought fit to withdraw, I think.

WORTHY: Withdraw! oons, sir! what d'ye mean by withdraw?

BRAZEN: I'll show you. (*Exit*)

WORTHY: She's lost, irrecoverably lost, and Plume's advice has ruined me! 'Sdeath! why should I, that knew her haughty spirit, be ruled by a man that's a stranger to her pride?

Enter PLUME.

PLUME: Ha, ha, ha! a battle-royal. Don't frown so, man; she's your own, I tell you; I saw the fury of her love in the extremity of her passion: the wildness of her anger is a certain sign that she loves you to madness. That rogue Kite began the battle with abundance of conduct, and will bring you off victorious, my life on't; he plays his part admirably; she's to be with him again presently.

WORTHY: But what could be the meaning of Brazen's familiarity with her?

PLUME: You are no logician, if you pretend to draw consequences from the actions of fools: there's no arguing by the rule of reason upon a science without principles, and such is their conduct. Whim, unaccountable whim, hurries 'em on like a man drunk with brandy before ten o'clock in the morning—But we lose our sport: Kite has opened above an hour ago; let's away.

Exeunt.

Act Four

SCENE THREE

A Chamber.
KITE, *disguised in a strange habit, sitting at a table, with books and globes.*

KITE: (*Rising*) By the position of the heavens, gained from my observation upon these celestial globes, I find that Luna was a tidewaiter, Sol a surveyor, Mercury a thief, Venus a whore, Saturn an alderman, Jupiter a rake, and Mars a serjeant of grenadiers; and this is the system of Kite the conjurer.

Enter PLUME *and* WORTHY.

PLUME: Well, what success?

KITE: I have sent away a shoemaker and a tailor already; one's to be a captain of marines, and the other a major of dragoons; I am to manage them at night.—Have you seen the lady, Mr Worthy?

WORTHY: Ay, but it won't do. Have you showed her her name, that I tore off from the bottom of the letter?

KITE: No, sir, I reserve that for the last stroke.

PLUME: What letter?

WORTHY: One that I would not let you see, for fear that you should break windows in good earnest.

Knocking at the door.

KITE: Officers, to your posts.

PLUME *and* WORTHY *conceal themselves behind a screen.*

Mind the door.

SERVANT *opens the door. Enter a* SMITH.

SMITH: Well, master, are you the cunning man?

Kite, of course, assumes a thick German accent for his impersonation, plus an intimidating mad-professor manner.

KITE: I am the learned Copernicus.

SMITH: Well, master, I'm but a poor man, and I can't afford above a shilling for my fortune.

KITE: Perhaps that is more than 'tis worth.

SMITH: Look'ee, doctor, let me have something that's good for my shilling, or I'll have my money again.

KITE: If there be faith in the stars, you shall have your shilling forty-fold.—Your hand, countryman.—You are by trade a smith.

SMITH: How the devil should you know that?

KITE: Because the devil and you are brother-tradesmen—you were born under Forceps.

SMITH: Forceps, what's that?

KITE: One of the signs. There's Leo, Sagittarius, Forceps, Furnes, Dixmude, Namur, Brussels, Charleroy, and so forth—twelve of 'em.—Let me see—did you ever make any bombs or cannon-bullets?

SMITH: Not I.

KITE: You either have or will. The stars have decreed that you shall be—I must have more money, sir, your fortune's great.

SMITH: Faith, doctor, I have no more.

KITE: O sir, I'll trust you, and take it out of your arrears.

SMITH: Arrears! what arrears?

KITE: The five hundred pound that's owing to you from the government.

SMITH: Owing me?

KITE: Owing you, sir.—Let me see your t'other hand.—I beg your pardon, it will be owing to you: and the rogue of an agent will demand fifty per cent. for a fortnight's advance.

SMITH: I'm in the clouds, doctor, all this while.

KITE: Sir, I am above 'em, among the stars. In two years, three months, and two hours, you will be made captain of the forges to the grand train of artillery, and will have ten shillings a day, and two servants. 'Tis the decree of the stars, and of the fixed stars, that are as immovable as your anvil; strike, sir, while the iron is hot. Fly, sir, begone!

SMITH: What, what would you have me do, doctor? I wish the stars would put me in a way for this fine place.

KITE: The stars do.—Let me see—ay, about an hour hence walk carelessly into the market-place, and you'll see a tall, slender gentleman, cheapening a penny-worth of apples, with a cane hanging upon his button. This gentleman will ask you what's o'clock. He's your man, and the maker of your fortune! Follow him, follow him.— And now go home, and take leave of your wife and children; an hour hence exactly is your time.

Plume, who is hidden behind a screen, brandishes his cane in front of Kite's face.

SMITH: A tall slender gentleman, you say, with a cane? Pray, what sort of head has the cane?

KITE: An amber head with a black ribbon.

SMITH: And pray of what employment is the gentleman?

KITE: Let me see; he's either a collector of the excise, a plenipotentiary, or a captain of grenadiers, I can't tell exactly which. But he'll call you honest—your name is—

SMITH: Thomas.

KITE: Right! He'll call you honest Tom.

SMITH: But how the devil should he know my name?

KITE: Oh, there are several sorts of Toms!
Tom 'o Lincoln, Tom-tit, Tom Tell-troth,
Tom o' Bedlam, and Tom Fool.

Knocking at the door.

—Begone!—an hour hence precisely.

SMITH: You say he'll ask me what's
o'clock?

KITE: Most certainly.—And you'll answer
you don't know:—and be sure you look at
St Mary's dial; for the sun won't shine, and
if it should, you won't be able to tell the
figures.

SMITH: I will, I will. (*Exit*)

The scene with the butcher was cut for reasons of time—it is self-contained and dramatically dispensable.

PLUME: (*Behind*) Well done, conjurer! go on and prosper.

KITE: As you were!

Enter a BUTCHER.

(*Aside*) What, my old friend Pluck the butcher! I offered the surly bull-dog five guineas this morning, and he refused it.

BUTCHER: So, Master Conjurer, here's half-a-crown.—And now you must understand—

KITE: Hold, friend, I know your business beforehand.

BUTCHER: You're devilish cunning then, for I don't well know it myself.

KITE: I know more than you, friend. You have a foolish saying, that such a one knows no more than the man in the moon: I tell you, the man in the moon knows more than all the men under the sun. Don't the moon see all the world?

BUTCHER: All the world see the moon, I must confess.

KITE: Then she must see all the world, that's certain.—Give me your hand.—You're by trade either a butcher or a surgeon.

BUTCHER: True, I am a butcher.

KITE: And a surgeon you will be, the employments differ only in the name: he that can cut up an ox, may dissect a man; and the same dexterity that cracks a marrow bone, will cut off a leg or an arm.

BUTCHER: What d'ye mean, doctor, what d'ye mean?

KITE: Patience, patience, Mr Surgeon-General; the stars are great bodies, and move slowly.

BUTCHER: But what d'ye mean by surgeon-general, doctor?

KITE: Nay, sir, if your worship won't have patience, I must beg the favour of your worship's absence.

BUTCHER: My worship! my worship! but why my worship?

KITE: Nay then, I have done. (*Sits down*)

BUTCHER: Pray doctor—

KITE: Fire and fury, sir!—(*Rises in a passion*) Do you think the stars will be hurried? Do the stars owe you any money, sir, that you dare to dun their lordships at this rate? Sir, I am porter to the stars, and I am ordered to let no dun come near their doors.

BUTCHER: Dear doctor, I never had any dealings with the stars, they don't owe me a penny. But since you are their porter, please to accept of this half-crown to drink their healths, and don't be angry.

KITE: Let me see your hand then once more.—Here has been gold—five guineas, my friend, in this very hand this morning.

BUTCHER: Nay, then he is the devil!—Pray, doctor, were you born of a woman? or did you come into the world of your own head?

KITE: That's a secret.—This gold was offered you by a proper handsome man, called Hawk, or Buzzard, or—

BUTCHER: Kite, you mean.

KITE: Ay, ay, Kite.

BUTCHER: As arrant a rogue as ever carried a halberd! The impudent rascal would have decoyed me for a soldier!

KITE: A soldier! A man of your substance for a soldier! Your mother has a hundred pound in hard money, lying at this minute in the hands of a mercer, not forty yards from this place.

BUTCHER: Oons! and so she has, but very few know so much.

KITE: I know it, and that rogue, what's his name, Kite, knew it, and offered you five guineas to list because he knew your poor mother would give the hundred for your discharge.

BUTCHER: There's a dog now!—'sflesh, doctor, I'll give you t'other half-crown, and tell me that this same Kite will be hanged.

KITE: He's in as much danger as any man in the county of Salop.

BUTCHER: There's your fee.—But you have forgot the surgeon-general all this while.

KITE: You put the stars in a passion.—(*Looks on his books*) But now they are pacified again:—Let me see, did you never cut off a man's leg?

BUTCHER: No.

KITE: Recollect, pray.

BUTCHER: I say, no.

KITE: That's strange! Wonderful strange! But nothing is strange to me, such wonderful changes have I seen.—The second, or third, ay, the third campaign that you make in Flanders, the leg of a great officer will be shattered by a great shot, you will be there accidentally, and with your cleaver chop off the limb at a blow: in short, the operation will be performed with so much dexterity, that with general applause you will be made surgeon-general of the whole army.

BUTCHER: Nay, for the matter of cutting off a limb, I'll do't, I'll do't with any surgeon in Europe; but I have no thoughts of making a campaign.

KITE: You have no thoughts? What's matter for your thoughts? The stars have decreed it, and you must go.

BUTCHER: The stars decree it! Oons, sir, the justices can't press me!

KITE: Nay, friend, 'tis none of my business —I have done; only mind this, you'll know more an hour and a half hence—that's all, farewell! (*Going*)

BUTCHER: Hold, hold, doctor!—Surgeon-general! what is the place worth pray?

KITE: Five hundred pounds a year, besides guineas for claps.

BUTCHER: Five hundred pounds a year!— An hour and a half hence, you say?

KITE: Prithee, friend, be quiet, don't be so troublesome. Here's such a work to make a booby butcher accept of five hundred pound a year! But if you must hear it—I tell you in short, you'll be standing in your stall an hour and half hence, and a gentleman will come by with a snuff-box in his hand, and the tip of his handkerchief hanging out of his right pocket; he'll ask you the price of a loin of veal, and at the same time stroke your great dog upon the head, and call him Chopper.

BUTCHER: Mercy on us! Chopper is the dog's name.

KITE: Look'ee there—what I say is true—things that are to come must come to pass. Get you home, sell off your stock, don't mind the whining and the snivelling of your mother and your sister—woman always hinder preferment—make what money you can, and follow that gentleman, his name begins with a P, mind that.—There will be the barber's daughter, too, that you promised marriage to—she will be pulling and hauling you to pieces.

BUTCHER: What! know Sally too? He's the devil, and he needs must go that the devil drives.—(*Going*) The tip of his handkerchief out of his left pocket?

KITE: No, no, his right pocket; if it be the left, 'tis none of the man.

BUTCHER: Well, well, I'll mind him. (*Exit*)

PLUME: (*Behind, with his pocket book*) The right pocket, you say?

KITE: I hear the rustling of silks.

Knocking at the door.

Fly, sir! 'tis Madam Melinda.

Enter MELINDA *and* LUCY.

Tycho, chairs for the ladies. (*Calls to servant*)

MELINDA: Don't trouble yourself, we sha'n't stay, doctor.

KITE: Your ladyship is to stay much longer than you imagine.

MELINDA: For what?

During the session with Melinda and Lucy, Plume hides under the table, supplying appropriate growls when Kite refers to the presence of the devil in the shape of a dog.

'Tycho' refers to Tycho Brahe (1546–1601), the celebrated Danish astronomer. The servant, present throughout the scene, is Kite's boy drummer from I.1, disguised as a hunchback imp.

KITE: For a husband.—(*To* LUCY) For your part, madam, you won't stay for a husband.

LUCY: Pray, doctor, do you converse with the stars, or the devil?

KITE: With both. When I have the destinies of men in search, I consult the stars; when the affairs of women come under my hands, I advise with my t'other friend.

MELINDA: And have you raised the devil upon my account?

KITE: Yes, madam, and he's now under the table.

LUCY: Oh, Heavens protect us! Dear madam, let's be gone.

KITE: If you be afraid of him, why do you come to consult him?

MELINDA: (*To* LUCY) Don't fear, fool.—
(*To* KITE) Do you think, sir, that because
I am a woman, I'm to be fooled out of my
reason, or frighted out of my senses?
Come, show me this devil.

KITE: He's a little busy at present; but when
he has done, he'll wait on you.

MELINDA: What is he doing?

KITE: Writing your name in his pocket-
book.

MELINDA: He, ha! my name! Pray, what
have you or he to do with my name?

KITE: Look'ee, fair lady, the devil is a very
modest person, he seeks nobody unless
they seek him first; he's chained up like a
mastiff, and can't stir unless he be let
loose. You come to me to have your fortune told—do you think, madam, that I can
answer you of my own head? No, madam,
the affairs of women are so irregular, that
nothing less than the devil can give any
account of 'em. Now to convince you of
your incredulity, I'll show you a trial of my
skill.—Here, you Cacodemo del Plumo—
exert your power, draw me this lady's
name, the word Melinda, in the proper
letters and character of her own handwrit-
ing.—Do it at three motions—one—two—
three—'tis done.—Now, madam, will you
please to send your maid to fetch it?

LUCY: I fetch it! The devil fetch me if I do!

MELINDA: My name in my own hand-
writing! That would be convincing indeed.

KITE: Seeing's believing.—(*Goes to the
table, lifts up the carpet*) Here, Tre, Tre,
poor Tre, give me the bone, sirrah.—
There's your name upon that square piece
of paper—behold!

MELINDA: 'Tis wonderful! my very letters
to a tittle!

LUCY: 'Tis like your hand, madam, but not
so like your hand neither, and now I look
nearer, 'tis not like your hand at all.

KITE: Here's a chambermaid now that will
outlie the devil!

**This and the following four speeches
were cut in performance, for reasons of
plot simplification. Lucy merely retains
the piece of paper for her own subsequent
use.**

102

LUCY: Look'ee, madam, they sha'n't impose upon us; people can't remember their hands, no more than they can their faces.— Come, madam, let us be certain: write your name upon this paper, then we'll compare the two names. (*Takes out a paper, and folds it*)

KITE: Anything for your satisfaction, madam—here's pen and ink.

MELINDA *writes,* LUCY *holds the paper.*

LUCY: Let me see it, madam. 'Tis the same —the very same.—(*Aside*) But I'll secure one copy for my own affairs.

MELINDA: This is demonstration.

KITE: 'Tis so, madam.—The word demonstration comes from Daemon, the father of lies.

MELINDA: Well, doctor, I am convinced; and now, pray, what account can you give me of my future fortune?

KITE: Before the sun has made one course round this earthly globe, your fortune will be fixed for happiness or misery.

MELINDA: What! so near the crisis of my fate!

KITE: Let me see—about the hour of ten to-morrow morning you will be saluted by a gentleman, who will come to take his leave of you, being designed for travel; his intention of going abroad is sudden, and the occasion a woman. Your fortune and his are like the bullet and the barrel, one runs plump into the other. In short, if the gentleman travels, he will die abroad; and if he does not, you will die before he comes home.

MELINDA: What sort of man is he?

KITE: Madam, he's a fine gentleman and a lover, that is, a man of very good sense, and a very great fool.

MELINDA: How is that possible, doctor?

KITE: Because, madam—because it is so.—A woman's reason is the best for a man's being a fool.

MELINDA: Ten o'clock, you say?

KITE: Ten—about the hour of tea-drinking throughout the kingdom.

MELINDA: Here, doctor.—(Gives money) Lucy, have you any questions to ask?

LUCY: O madam! a thousand.

KITE: I must beg your patience till another time; for I expect more company this minute; besides, I must discharge the gentleman under the table.

LUCY: Oh, pray, sir, discharge us first!

KITE: Tycho, wait on the ladies downstairs. Exeunt MELINDA and LUCY. PLUME and WORTHY come forward.

KITE: Mr Worthy, you were pleased to wish me joy to-day. I hope to be able to return the compliment to-morrow.

WORTHY: I'll make it the best compliment to you that ever I made in my life if you do. But I must be a traveller, you say?

KITE: No farther than the chops of the Channel, I presume, sir.

Brazen is not on top form in the final section of the scene, which merely adds two more letters to a plot already littered with correspondence. It was accordingly decided to cut it.

PLUME: That we have concerted already.—
Loud knocking at the door.
Heyday! you don't profess mid-wifery, doctor.

KITE: Away to your ambuscade!
PLUME and WORTHY retire as before. Enter BRAZEN.

BRAZEN: Your servant, servant, my dear.

KITE: Stand off, I have my familiar already.

BRAZEN: Are you bewitched, my dear?

KITE: Yes, my dear; but mine is a peaceable spirit, and hates gunpowder. Thus I fortify myself.—(*Draws a circle round him*) And now, Captain, have a care how you force my lines.

BRAZEN: Lines! what dost talk of lines! You have something like a fishing-rod there, indeed; but I come to be acquainted with you, man.—What's your name, my dear?

KITE: Conundrum.

BRAZEN: Conundrum! Rat me, I knew a famous doctor in London of your name!— Where were you born?

KITE: I was born in Algebra.

BRAZEN: Algebra! 'tis no country in Christendom, I'm sure, unless it be some place in the Highlands in Scotland.

KITE: Right! I told you I was bewitched.

BRAZEN: So am I, my dear: I am going to be married. I have had two letters from a lady of fortune that loves me to madness, fits, colic, spleen, and vapours. Shall I marry her in four-and-twenty hours, yea, or no?

KITE: I must have the year and day of the month when these letters were dated.

BRAZEN: Why, you old bitch, did you ever hear of love-letters dated with the year and day o' the month? Do you think billets-doux are like bank bills?

KITE: They are not so good.—But if they bear no date, I must examine the contents.

BRAZEN: Contents! that you shall, old boy: here they be both. (*Pulls out two letters*)

KITE: Only the last you received, if you please.—(*Takes one of the letters*) Now, sir, if you please to let me consult my books for a minute, I'll send this letter inclosed to you with the determination of the stars upon it, to your lodgings.

BRAZEN: With all my heart—I must give him—(*Puts his hand in his pocket*) Algebra! I fancy, doctor, 'tis hard to calculate the place of your nativity?—Here.—(*Gives him money*) And if I succeed, I'll build a watchtower upon the top of the highest mountain in Wales for the study of astrology, and the benefit of Conundrums. (*Exit*)

PLUME *and* WORTHY *come forward.*

WORTHY: O doctor! that letter's worth a million. Let me see it.—(*Takes the letter*) And now I have it, I am afraid to open it.

PLUME: Pho! let me see it.—(*Snatches the letter from* WORTHY *and opens it*) If she be a jilt—damn her, she is one! there's her name at the bottom on't.

WORTHY: How! then I'll travel in good earnest.—(*Looking at the letter*) By all my hopes, 'tis Lucy's hand!

PLUME: Lucy's!

WORTHY: Certainly; 'tis no more like Melinda's character than black is to white.

PLUME: Then 'tis certainly Lucy's contrivance to draw in Brazen for a husband.— But are you sure 'tis not Melinda's hand?

WORTHY: You shall see.—(*To* KITE) Where's the bit of paper I gave you just now that the devil writ Melinda upon?

KITE: Here, sir.

PLUME: 'Tis plain they're not the same. And is this the malicious name that was subscribed to the letter, which made Mr Balance send his daughter into the country?

WORTHY: The very same: the other fragments I showed you just now.

PLUME: But 'twas barbarous to conceal this so long, and to continue me so many hours in the pernicious heresy of believing that angelic creature could change!—Poor Silvia!

WORTHY: Rich Silvia you mean, and poor captain, ha, ha, ha! Come, come, friend, Melinda is true and shall be mine; Silvia is constant, and may be yours.

PLUME: No, she's above my hopes: but for her sake I'll recant my opinion of her sex.

By some the sex is blamed without design,
Light harmless censure, such as yours and
    mine,
Sallies of wit, and vapours of our wine.
Others the justice of the sex condemn,
And wanting merit to create esteem,
Would hide their own defects by censuring
    them.
But they, secure in their all-conquering
    charms,
Laugh at the vain efforts of false alarms;
He magnifies their conquests who
    complains,
For none would struggle were they not in
    chains.

Exeunt.

Act Five

SCENE ONE

Performed in the bedroom itself, and mostly on the bed.

An Anteroom adjoining SILVIA'S *Bedchamber; a periwig, hat, and sword, upon the table.*
SILVIA *discovered in her nightcap.*

SILVIA: I have rested but indifferently, and I believe my bedfellow was as little pleased as I.

ROSE *awakens.*

Good morrow, my dear, how d'ye this morning?

ROSE: Just as I was last night, neither better nor worse for you.

SILVIA: What's the matter? Did you not like your bedfellow?

ROSE: I don't know whether I had a bedfellow or not.

SILVIA: Did not I lie with you?

ROSE: No—I wonder you could have the conscience to ruin a poor girl for nothing.

SILVIA: I have saved thee from ruin, child; don't be melancholy, I can give you as many fine things as the captain can.

ROSE: But you can't, I'm sure.

Knocking at the door.

SILVIA: Odso! my accoutrements.—(*Puts on her periwig, hat and sword*) Who's at the door?

CONSTABLE: (*Without*) Open the door, or we'll break it down.

SILVIA: Patience a little—(*Opens the door*)

Enter CONSTABLE *and* MOB.

The constable is played as a smug and officious bureaucrat.

CONSTABLE: We have 'um, we have 'um! the duck and the mallard both in the decoy.

108

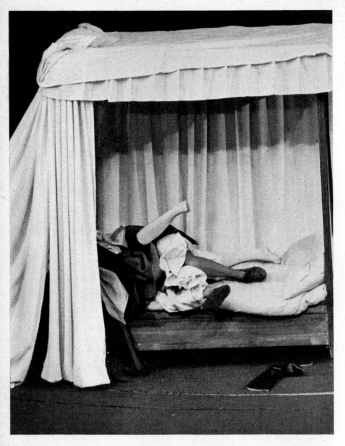

Silvia's plot here looks like succeeding: she is to appear in court before her father, who will presumably order her into the army—with Plume.

SILVIA: What means this riot? Stand off!— (*Draws*) The man dies that comes within reach of my point.

CONSTABLE: That is not the point, master; put up your sword or I shall knock you down; and so I command the Queen's peace.

SILVIA: You are some blockhead of a constable.

CONSTABLE: I am so, and have a warrant to apprehend the bodies of you and your whore there.

ROSE: Whore! Never was poor woman so abused.

Enter BULLOCK unbuttoned.

BULLOCK: What's the matter now?—O Mr Bridewell! what brings you abroad so early?

CONSTABLE: This, sir.—(*Lays hold of BULLOCK*) You're the Queen's prisoner.

BULLOCK: Wauns, you lie, sir! I'm the Queen's soldier.

CONSTABLE: No matter for that, you shall go before Justice Balance.

SILVIA: Balance! 'tis what I wanted.—Here, Mr Constable, I resign my sword.

ROSE: Can't you carry us before the captain, Mr Bridewell?

CONSTABLE: Captain! han't you got your bellyfull of captains yet?—Come, come, make way there.

Exeunt.

Act Five

SCENE TWO

Justice BALANCE's *House.*
Enter BALANCE *and* SCALE.

SCALE: I say 'tis not to be borne, Mr Balance!

BALANCE: Look'ee, Mr Scale, for my own part I shall be very tender in what regards the officers of the army; they expose their lives to so many dangers for us abroad, that we may give them some grain of allowance at home.

SCALE: Allowance! This poor girl's father is my tenant; and, if I mistake not, her mother nursed a child for you. Shall they debauch our daughters to our faces?

BALANCE: Consider, Mr Scale, that were it not for the bravery of these officers, we should have French dragoons among us, that would leave us neither liberty, property, wife, nor daughter. Come, Mr Scale, the gentlemen are vigorous and warm, and may they continue so; the same heat that stirs them up to love, spurs them on to battle; you never knew a great general in your life, that did not love a whore. This I only speak in reference to Captain Plume— for the other spark I know nothing of.

SCALE: Nor can I hear of anybody that does.—Oh, here they come.

Enter SILVIA, BULLOCK, *and* ROSE, *prisoners;* CONSTABLE *and* MOB.

CONSTABLE: May it please your worships we took them in the very act, re infecta, sir. The gentleman, indeed, behaved himself like a gentleman; for he drew his sword and swore, and afterwards laid it down and said nothing.

BALANCE: Give the gentleman his sword again—wait you without.—

Exeunt CONSTABLE *and* MOB.

I'm sorry, sir,—(*To* SILVIA) to know a gentleman upon such terms, that the occasion of our meeting should prevent the satisfaction of an acquaintance.

SILVIA: Sir, you need make no apology for your warrant, no more than I shall do for my behaviour: my innocence is upon an equal foot with your authority.

SCALE: Innocence! Have not you seduced that young maid?

SILVIA: No, Mr Goosecap, she seduced me.

BULLOCK: So she did, I'll swear—for she proposed marriage first.

BALANCE: What! then you are married, child? (*To* ROSE)

ROSE: Yes, sir, to my sorrow.

BALANCE: Who was witness?

BULLOCK: That was I—I danced, threw the stocking, and spoke jokes by their bedside, I'm sure.

BALANCE: Who was the minister?

BULLOCK: Minister! we are soldiers, and want no minister. They were married by the Articles of War.

BALANCE: Hold thy prating, fool!—(*To* SILVIA) Your appearance, sir, promises some understanding; pray what does this fellow mean?

SILVIA: He means marriage, I think—but that, you know, is so odd a thing, that hardly any two people under the sun agree in the ceremony; some make it a sacrament, others a convenience, and others make it a jest; but among soldiers 'tis most sacred. Our sword, you know, is our honour; that we lay down; the hero jumps over it first, and the amazon after—leap rogue, follow whore—the drum beats a ruff, and so to bed; that's all—the cere-

mony is concise.

BULLOCK: And the prettiest ceremony, so full of pastime and prodigality!

BALANCE: What! are you a soldier?

BULLOCK: Ay, that I am. Will your worship lend me your cane, and I'll show you how I can exercise.

BALANCE: (*Striking him over the head*) Take it.—(*To* SILVIA) Pray, sir, what commission may you bear?

SILVIA: I'm called captain, sir, by all the coffeemen, drawers, whores, and groom-porters in London; for I wear a red coat, a sword, a hat bien trousse, a martial twist in my cravat, a fierce knot in my periwig, a cane upon my button, piquet in my head, and dice in my pocket.

SCALE: Your name, pray, sir?

SILVIA: Captain Pinch: I cock my hat with a pinch, I take snuff with a pinch, pay my whores with a pinch. In short, I can do anything at a pinch, but fight and fill my belly.

BALANCE: And pray, sir, what brought you into Shropshire?

SILVIA: A pinch, sir: I knew you country gentlemen want wit, and you know that we town gentlemen want money, and so—

BALANCE: I understand you, sir.—Here, constable!

Re-enter CONSTABLE.

Take this gentleman into custody till farther orders.

ROSE: Pray, your worship, don't be uncivil to him, for he did me no hurt; he's the most harmless man in the world, for all he talks so.

SCALE: Come, come, child, I'll take care of you.

SILVIA: What, gentlemen! Rob me of my freedom, and my wife at once! 'Tis the first time they ever went together.

BALANCE: Heark'ee, constable! (*Whispers him*)

CONSTABLE: It shall be done, sir.—Come along, sir.

Exit with BULLOCK, ROSE *and* SILVIA.

BALANCE: Come, Mr Scale, we'll manage the spark presently.

Exeunt.

Act Five

SCENE THREE

A table is set for tea, which is served in china bowls, not tea-cups.

The first six speeches have an obvious sub-text. Ostensibly talking about travel, Melinda and Worthy are actually blaming each other for the wretched state of their love affair.

MELINDA's *Apartment*.

Enter MELINDA *and* WORTHY.

MELINDA: (*Aside*) So far the prediction is right, 'tis ten exactly.—(*Aloud*) And pray, sir, how long have you been in this travelling humour?

WORTHY: 'Tis natural, madam, for us to avoid what disturbs our quiet.

MELINDA: Rather the love of change, which is more natural, may be the occasion of it.

WORTHY: To be sure, madam, there must be charms in variety, else neither you nor I should be so fond of it.

MELINDA: You mistake, Mr Worthy, I am not so fond of variety as to travel for't, nor do I think it prudence in you to run yourself into a certain expense and danger, in hopes of precarious pleasures, which at best never answer expectation; as 'tis evident from the example of most travellers, that long more to return to their own country than they did to go abroad.

WORTHY: What pleasures I may receive abroad are indeed uncertain; but this I am sure of, I shall meet with less cruelty among the most barbarous nations than I have found at home.

MELINDA: Come, sir, you and I have been jangling a great while; I fancy if we made up our accounts, we should the sooner come to an agreement.

WORTHY: Sure, madam, you won't dispute your being in my debt? My fears, sighs, vows, promises, assiduities, anxieties, jealousies, have run on for a whole year,

without any payment.

MELINDA: A year! Oh, Mr Worthy! what you owe to me is not to be paid under a seven years' servitude. How did you use me the year before? when, taking the advantage of my innocence and necessity, you would have made me your mistress, that is, your slave. Remember the wicked insinuations, artful baits, deceitful arguments, cunning pretences; then your impudent behaviour, loose expressions, familiar letters, rude visits,—remember those! those, Mr Worthy!

WORTHY: (*Aside*) I do remember, and am sorry I made no better use of 'em.—(*Aloud*) But you may remember, madam, that—

MELINDA: Sir, I'll remember nothing—'tis your interest that I should forget: you have been barbarous to me, I have been cruel to you; put that and that together, and let one balance the other. Now if you will begin upon a new score, lay aside your adventuring airs, and behave yourself handsomely till Lent be over; here's my hand, I'll use you as a gentleman should be.

WORTHY: And if I don't use you as a gentlewoman should be, may this be my poison. (*Kissing her hand*)

Enter SERVANT.

SERVANT: Madam, the coach is at the door. (*Exit*)

MELINDA: I am going to Mr Balance's country-house to see my cousin Silvia; I have done her an injury, and can't be easy till I have asked her pardon.

WORTHY: I dare not hope for the honour of waiting on you.

MELINDA: My coach is full; but if you will be so gallant as to mount your own horses and follow us, we shall be glad to be overtaken; and if you bring Captain Plume with you, we sha'n't have the worse reception.

WORTHY: I'll endeavour it.

Exit, leading MELINDA.

Act Five

SCENE FOUR

The Market-place.

Enter PLUME *and* KITE.

PLUME: A baker, a tailor, a smith, and a butcher—I believe the first colony planted in Virginia had not more trades in their company than I have in mine.

KITE: The butcher, sir, will have his hands full; for we have two sheep-stealers among us. I hear of a fellow, too, committed just now for stealing of horses.

PLUME: We'll dispose of him among the dragoons. Have we ne'er a poulterer among us?

KITE: Yes, sir, the king of the gipsies is a very good one, he has an excellent hand at a goose or a turkey.—Here's Captain Brazen, sir; I must go look after the men. (*Exit*)

Enter BRAZEN, *reading a letter.*

BRAZEN: Um, um, um, the canonical hour —Um, um, very well.—My dear Plume! give me a buss.

PLUME: Half a score, if you will, my dear. What hast got in thy hand, child?

BRAZEN: 'Tis a project for laying out a thousand pound.

PLUME: Were it not requisite to project first how to get it in?

BRAZEN: You can't imagine, my dear, that I want twenty thousand pound; I have spent twenty times as much in the service. Now, my dear, pray advise me, my head runs much upon architecture; shall I build a privateer or a playhouse?

'Half a score' is literally interpreted: they kiss ten times at top speed.

118

PLUME: An odd question—a privateer, or a playhouse! 'Twill require some consideration.—Faith, I'm for a privateer.

BRAZEN: I'm not of your opinion, my dear.—For in the first place a privateer may be ill built.

PLUME: And so may a playhouse.

BRAZEN: But a privateer may be ill manned.

PLUME: And so may a playhouse.

BRAZEN: But a privateer may run upon the shallows.

PLUME: Not so often as a playhouse.

BRAZEN: But you know a privateer may spring a leak.

PLUME: And I know that a playhouse may spring a great many.

BRAZEN: But suppose the privateer comes home with a rich booty, we should never agree about our shares.

PLUME: 'Tis just so in a playhouse:—so, by my advice, you shall fix upon the privateer.

BRAZEN: Agreed!—But if this twenty thousand should not be in specie—

PLUME: What twenty thousand?

BRAZEN: Heark'ee. (*Whispers*)

PLUME: Married!

BRAZEN: Presently, we're to meet about half a mile out of town at the water-side—and so forth.—(*Reads*) For fear I should be known by any of Worthy's friends, you must give me leave to wear my mask till after the ceremony, which will make me for ever yours.—Look'ee there, my dear dog. (*Shows the bottom of the letter to* PLUME)

PLUME: Melinda!—and by this light, her own hand!—Once more, if you please, my dear.—Her hand exactly—Just now, you say?

BRAZEN: This minute I must be gone.

PLUME: Have a little patience, and I'll go with you.

BRAZEN: No, no, I see a gentleman coming this way, that may be inquisitive; 'tis Worthy, do you know him?

PLUME: By sight only.

BRAZEN: Have a care, the very eyes discover secrets. (*Exit*)

Enter WORTHY.

WORTHY: To boot and saddle, captain! you must mount.

PLUME: Whip and spur, Worthy, or you won't mount.

WORTHY: But I shall: Melinda and I are agreed, she's gone to visit Silvia, we are to mount and follow; and could we carry a parson with us, who knows what might be done for us both?

PLUME: Don't trouble your head; Melinda has secured a parson already.

WORTHY: Already! Do you know more than I?

PLUME: Yes, I saw it under her hand.— Brazen and she are to meet half a mile hence at the water-side, there to take boat, I suppose to be ferried over to the Elysian fields, if there by any such thing in matrimony.

Worthy's speech about Lucy and Plume's reply were omitted, since they relate to passages already cut in IV, 3.

WORTHY: I parted with Melinda just now; she assured me she hated Brazen, and that she resolved to discard Lucy for daring to write letters to him in her name.

PLUME: Nay, nay, there's nothing of Lucy in this—I tell ye, I saw Melinda's hand, as surely as this is mine.

WORTHY: But I tell you she's gone this minute to Justice Balance's country-house.

PLUME: But I tell you she's gone this minute to the water-side.

Enter SERVANT.

SERVANT: (*To* WORTHY) Madam Melinda has sent word that you need not trouble yourself to follow her because her journey to Justice Balance's is put off, and she's gone to take the air another way.

WORTHY: How! her journey put off!

PLUME: That is, her journey was a put-off to you.

WORTHY: 'Tis plain, plain!—But how, where, when is she to meet Brazen?

PLUME: Just now, I tell you, half a mile hence, at the water-side.

WORTHY: Up or down the water?

PLUME: That I don't know.

WORTHY: I'm glad my horses are ready. —Jack, get 'em out.

Exit SERVANT.

PLUME: Shall I go with you?

WORTHY: Not an inch; I shall return presently.

PLUME: You'll find me at the hall; the justices are sitting by this time, and I must attend them.

Exeunt severally.

Act Five

SCENE FIVE

In performance this scene and V.6 were transposed, in order to round off the Melinda–Worthy sub-plot before getting to the court scene and the resolution of the Plume–Silvia relationship.

A Court of Justice.
BALANCE, SCALE *and* SCRUPLE *upon the bench*; KITE *and* CONSTABLE *advance forward.*

KITE: Pray, who are those honourable gentlemen upon the bench?

CONSTABLE: He in the middle is Justice Balance, he on the right is Justice Scale, and he on the left is Justice Scruple; and I am Mr Constable:—four very honest gentlemen.

KITE: O dear, Sir! I am your most obedient servant.—(*Saluting him*) I fancy, sir, that your employment and mine are much the same; for my business is to keep people in order, and if they disobey, to knock 'em down; and then we are both staff-officers.

CONSTABLE: Nay, I'm a serjeant myself—of the militia. Come, brother, you shall see me exercise. Suppose this a musket now: now I am shouldered. (*Puts his staff on his right shoulder*)

KITE: Ay, you are shouldered pretty well for a constable's staff; but for a musket, you must put it on t'other shoulder, my dear.

CONSTABLE: Adso! that's true.—Come, now give the word of command.

KITE: Silence!

CONSTABLE: Ay, ay, so we will—we will be silent.

KITE: Silence, you dog, silence! (*Strikes him over the head with his halberd*)

CONSTABLE: That's the way to silence a man with a witness! What d'ye mean, friend?

KITE: Only to exercise you, sir.

CONSTABLE: Your exercise differs so from ours, that we shall ne'er agree about it. If my own captain had given me such a rap, I had taken the law of him.

Enter PLUME.

BALANCE: Captain, you're welcome.

PLUME: Gentlemen, I thank you.

SCRUPLE: Come, honest Captain, sit by me.—

PLUME *ascends and sits upon the bench.*

Now produce your prisoners.—Here, that fellow there—set him up.—Mr Constable, what have you to say against this man?

CONSTABLE: I have nothing to say against him, an please you.

BALANCE: No? What made you bring him hither?

CONSTABLE: I don't know, an please your worship.

SCALE: Did not the contents of your warrant direct what sort of men to take up?

CONSTABLE: I can't tell, an please ye; I can't read.

SCRUPLE: A very pretty constable truly!— I find we have no business here.

KITE: May it please the worshipful bench, I desire to be heard in this case, as being counsel for the Queen.

BALANCE: Come, serjeant, you shall be heard, since nobody else will speak; we won't come here for nothing.

KITE: This man is but one man; the country may spare him, and the army wants him; besides, he's cut out by nature for a grenadier; he's five foot ten inches high; he shall box, wrestle, or dance the Cheshire Round with any man in the country; he gets drunk every sabbath day, and he beats his wife.

WIFE: You lie, sirrah! you lie!—An please your worship, he's the best natur'dst, pains-taking'st man in the parish, witness my five poor children.

SCRUPLE: A wife and five children!—You, constable, you rogue, how durst you impress a man that has a wife and five children?

SCALE: Discharge him! discharge him!

BALANCE: Hold, gentlemen!—Hark'ee, friend, how do you maintain your wife and children?

PLUME: They live upon wildfowl and venison, sir; the husband keeps a gun, and kills all the hares and partridges within five miles round.

BALANCE: A gun! nay, if he be so good at gunning, he shall have enough on't. He may be of use against the French, for he shoots flying, to be sure.

SCRUPLE: But his wife and children, Mr Balance!

WIFE: Ay, ay, that's the reason you would send him away; you know I have a child every year, and you are afraid they should come upon the parish at last.

PLUME: Look'ee there, gentlemen, the honest woman has spoke it at once; the parish had better maintain five children this year, then six or seven the next. That fellow, upon his high feeding, may get you two or three beggars at a birth.

WIFE: Look'ee, Mr Captain, the parish shall get nothing by sending him away, for I won't lose my teeming-time, if there be a man left in the parish.

BALANCE: Send that woman to the house of correction—and the man—

KITE: I'll take care o' him, if you please. (*Takes him down*)

SCALE: Here, you constable, the next:— set up that black-faced fellow, he has a gunpowder look. What can you say against this man, constable?

CONSTABLE: Nothing, but that he is a very honest man.

PLUME: Pray, gentlemen, let me have one

honest man in my company, for the novelty's sake.

BALANCE: What are you, friend?

MOB: A collier; I work in the coal-pits.

SCRUPLE: Look'ee, gentlemen, this fellow has a trade, and the Act of Parliament here expresses, that we are to impress no man that has any visible means of a livelihood.

KITE: May it please your worships, this man has no visible means of livelihood, for he works underground.

PLUME: Well said, Kite! Besides, the army wants miners.

BALANCE: Right, and had we an order of government for't, we could raise you in this, and the neighbouring county of Stafford, five hundred colliers, that would run you underground like moles, and do more service in a siege than all the miners in the army.

SCRUPLE: Well, friend, what have you to say for yourself?

MOB: I'm married.

KITE: Lack-a-day, so am I.

MOB: Here's my wife, poor woman.

BALANCE: Are you married, good woman?

WOMAN: I'm married in conscience.

KITE: May it please your worship, she's with child in conscience.

SCALE: Who married you, mistress?

WOMAN: My husband—we agreed that I should call him husband to avoid passing for a whore, and that he should call me wife to shun going for a soldier.

SCRUPLE: A very pretty couple! Pray, captain, will you take 'em both?

PLUME: What say you, Mr Kite? will you take care of the woman?

KITE: Yes, sir; she shall go with us to the seaside, and there, if she has a mind to drown herself, we'll take care that nobody shall hinder her.

BALANCE: Here, constable, bring in my man.—

Exit CONSTABLE.

Now, Captain, I'll fit you with a man, such as you ne'er listed in your life.

Re-enter CONSTABLE *with* SILVIA.

Oh! my friend Pinch, I'm very glad to see you.

SILVIA: Well, sir, and what then?

SCALE: What then! is that your respect to the bench?

SILVIA: Sir, I don't care a farthing for you nor your bench neither.

SCRUPLE: Look'ee, gentlemen, that's enough: he's a very impudent fellow, and fit for a soldier.

SCALE: A notorious rogue, I say, and very fit for a soldier.

CONSTABLE: A whoremaster, I say, and therefore fit to go.

BALANCE: What think you, captain?

PLUME: I think he's a very pretty fellow, and therefore fit to serve.

SILVIA: Me for a soldier! Send your own lazy, lubberly sons at home, fellows that hazard their necks every day in pursuit of a fox, yet dare not peep abroad to look an enemy in the face.

CONSTABLE: May it please your worships, I have a woman at the door to swear a rape against this rogue.

SILVIA: Is it your wife or daughter, booby? I ravished 'em both yesterday.

BALANCE: Pray, captain, read the Articles of War, we'll see him listed immediately.

PLUME: (*Reads*) Articles of War against mutiny and desertion—

SILVIA: Hold, sir!—Once more, gentlemen, have a care what you do, for you shall severely smart for any violence you offer to me; and you, Mr Balance, I speak to you particularly, you shall heartily repent it.

PLUME: Look'ee, young spark, say but one word more, and I'll build a horse for you as high as the ceiling, and make you rise the most tiresome journey that ever you made in your life.

SILVIA: You have made a fine speech, good Captain Huffcap, but you had better be quiet; I shall find a way to cool your courage.

PLUME: Pray, gentlemen, don't mind him, he's distracted.

SILVIA: 'Tis false! I am descended of as good a family as any in your country; my father is as good a man as any upon your bench, and I am heir to twelve hundred pounds a year.

BALANCE: He's certainly mad!—Pray, Captain, read the Articles of War.

SILVIA: Hold once more!—Pray, Mr Balance, to you I speak: suppose I were your child, would you use me at this rate?

BALANCE: No, faith, were you mine, I would send you to Bedlam first, and into the army afterwards.

SILVIA: But consider my father, sir: he's as good, as generous, as brave, as just a man as ever served his country; I'm his only child, perhaps the loss of me may break his heart.

BALANCE: He's a very great fool if it does. —Captain, if you don't list him this minute, I'll leave the court.

PLUME: Kite, do you distribute the levy-money to the men while I read.

KITE: Ay, sir.—Silence, gentlemen!

PLUME *reads the Articles of War.*

As Plume reads—at high speed—the Articles of War, a low and menacing drum-roll is heard offstage.

The extracts used in performance were the following:

No man shall presume so far as to raise or cause the least mutiny or Sedition in the Army, upon Pain of Death. And if any

BALANCE: Very well; now, Captain, let me beg the favour of you, not to discharge this fellow upon any account whatsoever, —Bring in the rest.

CONSTABLE: There are no more, an't please your worship.

BALANCE: No more! there were five two hours ago.

number of Soldiers shall presume to assemble amongst themselves for the demanding of their pay or shall at any time demand their pay in a mutinous manner, the soldiers shall be punished by **Death.**

No Officer or Soldier shall utter any Words leading to Sedition or Mutiny upon Pain of Death. And whosoever shall hear any Mutinous or Seditious Words spoken and shall not with all possible speed reveal the same to his Superior Officers, shall likewise be punished with Death.

If any Inferior Officer or Soldier shall refuse to obey his Superior Officer, he shall be punished with Death.

If any Officer or Soldier shall presume to resist any Officer in the Execution of his Office, or shall strike, or lift up his hand to strike, or shall draw, or lift up any weapon against his Superior Officer upon any pretence whatsoever, he shall suffer Death.

When any march is to be made, every Man who is sworn shall follow his Colours, and whoever shall without leave stay behind, or depart above a mile from the Camp, or out of the Army without Licence, shall die for it.

SILVIA: 'Tis true, sir; but this rogue of a constable let the rest escape for a bribe of eleven shillings a man; because he said the Act allowed him but ten, so the odd shilling was clear gains.

JUSTICES: How!

SILVIA: Gentlemen, he offered to let me get away for two guineas, but I had not so much about me. This is truth, and I'm ready to swear it.

KITE: And I'll swear it; give me the book. 'tis for the good of the service.

MOB: May it please your worship, I gave him half-a-crown to say that I was an honest man; but now, since that your worships have made me a rogue, I hope I shall have my money again.

BALANCE: 'Tis my opinion that this constable be put into the captain's hands, and if his friends don't bring four good men for his ransom by to-morrow night—Captain, you shall carry him to Flanders.

SCALE:
SCRUPLE:} Agreed! agreed!

PLUME: Mr Kite, take the constable into custody.

KITE: Ay, ay, sir.—(*To* CONSTABLE) Will you please to have your office taken from you? or will you handsomely lay down your staff, as your betters have done before you?

CONSTABLE *drops his staff.*

BALANCE: Come, gentlemen, there needs no great ceremony in adjourning this court.—Captain, you shall dine with me.

KITE: (*To* CONSTABLE) Come, Mr Militia Serjeant, I shall silence you now, I believe, without your taking the law of me.

Exeunt omnes.

Act Five

SCENE SIX

The Fields.
Enter BRAZEN *leading in* LUCY, *masked.*

BRAZEN: The boat is just below here.

Enter WORTHY *with a case of pistols under his arm.*

WORTHY: Here, sir, take your choice. (*Going between them and offering the pistols*)

BRAZEN: What! pistols! Are they charged, my dear?

WORTHY: With a brace of bullets each.

BRAZEN: But I'm a foot-officer, my dear, and never use pistols. The sword is my way—and I won't be put out of my road to please any man.

WORTHY: Nor I neither; so have at you. (*Cocks one pistol*)

BRAZEN: Look'ee, my dear, I don't care for pistols.—Pray, oblige me, and let us have a bout at sharps; damn it, there's no parrying these bullets!

WORTHY: Sir, if you han't your bellyfull of these, the swords shall come in for second course.

BRAZEN: Why, then, fire and fury! I have eaten smoke from the mouth of a cannon, sir; don't think I fear powder, for I live upon't. Let me see—(*Takes one*) And now, sir, how many paces distant shall we fire?

WORTHY: Fire you when you please, I'll reserve my shot till I'm sure of you.

BRAZEN: Come, where's your cloak?

WORTHY: Cloak! what d'ye mean?

BRAZEN: To fight upon; I always fight upon a cloak, 'tis our way abroad.

LUCY: Come, gentlemen, I'll end the strife. (*Unmasks*)

WORTHY: Lucy!—take her.

BRAZEN: The devil take me if I do! Huzza! —(*Fires his pistol*) D'ye hear, d'ye hear, you plaguy harridan, how those bullets whistle! Suppose they had been lodged in my gizzard now!

LUCY: Pray, sir, pardon me.

BRAZEN: I can't tell, child, till I know whether my money be safe.—(*Searching in his pockets*) Yes, yes, I do pardon you, but if I had you in the Rose Tavern, Covent Garden, with three or four hearty rakes, and three or four smart napkins, I would tell you another story, my dear. (*Exit*)

For "she wrote her name", read "the devil wrote her name"—to conform with the changes made in IV, 3.

WORTHY: And was Melinda privy to this?

LUCY: No, sir, she wrote her name upon a piece of paper at the fortune-teller's last night, which I put in my pocket, and writ above it to the captain.

WORTHY: And how came Melinda's journey put off?

LUCY: At the town's end she met Mr Balance's steward, who told her that Mrs Silvia was gone from her father's, and nobody could tell whither.

WORTHY: Silvia gone from her father's! This will be news to Plume.—Go home, and tell your lady how near I was being shot for her.

Exeunt severally.

Act Five

SCENE SEVEN

Justice BALANCE's *House.*
Enter BALANCE, *with a napkin in his hand,
as risen from dinner, and* STEWARD.

STEWARD: We did not miss her till the evening, sir; and then, searching for her in the chamber that was my young master's, we found her clothes there; but the suit that your son left in the press, when he went to London, was gone.

BALANCE: The white trimmed with silver?

STEWARD: The same.

BALANCE: You han't told that circumstance to anybody?

STEWARD: To none but your worship.

BALANCE: And be sure you don't. Go into the dining-room and tell Captain Plume that I beg to speak with him.

STEWARD: I shall. (*Exit*)

BALANCE: Was ever man so imposed upon! I had her promise, indeed, that she should never dispose of herself without my consent. I have consented with a witness, given her away as my act and deed. And this, I warrant, the captain thinks will pass! No, I shall never pardon him the villainy, first of robbing me of my daughter, and then the mean opinion he must have of me, to think that I could be so wretchedly imposed upon. Her extravagant passion might encourage her in the attempt, but the contrivance must be his. I'll know the truth presently.

Enter PLUME.

Pray, Captain, what have you done with your young gentleman soldier?

PLUME: He's at my quarters, I suppose, with the rest of my men.

BALANCE: Does he keep company with the common soldiers?

PLUME: No, he's generally with me.

BALANCE: He lies with you, I presume!

PLUME: No, faith, I offered him part of my bed; but the young rogue fell in love with Rose, and has lain with her, I think, since he came to town.

BALANCE: So that, between you both, Rose has been finely managed.

PLUME: Upon my honour, sir, she had no harm from me.

BALANCE: (*Aside*) All's safe, I find!— (*Aloud*) Now, Captain, you must know that the young fellow's impudence in court was well grounded; he said I should heartily repent his being listed, and so I do from my soul.

PLUME: Aye! For what reason?

BALANCE: Because he is no less than what he said he was, born of as good a family as any in this country, and is heir to twelve hundred pounds a year.

PLUME: I'm very glad to hear it—for I wanted but a man of that quality to make my company a perfect representative of the whole commons of England.

BALANCE: Won't you discharge him?

PLUME: Not under a hundred pound sterling.

BALANCE: You shall have it, for his father is my intimate friend.

PLUME: Then you shall have him for nothing.

BALANCE: Nay, sir, you shall have your price.

PLUME: Not a penny, sir; I value an obligation to you much above a hundred pound.

BALANCE: Perhaps, sir, you sha'n't repent your generosity.—Will you please to write his discharge in my pocket-book?—(*Gives his book*) In the meantime, we'll send for the gentleman—Who waits there?

Enter SERVANT.

Go to the Captain's lodging and inquire for Mr Wilful; tell him his captain wants him here immediately.

SERVANT: Sir, the gentleman's below at the door, inquiring for the captain.

PLUME: Bid him come up.—

Exit SERVANT.

Here's the discharge, sir.

BALANCE: Sir, I thank you.—(*Aside*) 'Tis plain he had no hand in't.

Enter SILVIA.

SILVIA: I think, Captain, you might have used me better than to leave me yonder among your swearing drunken crew. And you, Mr Justice, might have been so civil as to have invited me to dinner, for I have eaten with as good a man as your worship.

PLUME: Sir, you must charge our want of respect upon our ignorance of your quality. —But now you are at liberty—I have discharged you.

SILVIA: Discharged me!

BALANCE: Yes, sir, and you must once more go home to your father.

SILVIA: My father! then I am discovered.— O sir! (*Kneeling*) I expect no pardon.

BALANCE: Pardon! No, no, child, your crime shall be your punishment.—Here, Captain, I deliver her over to the conjugal power for her chastisement; since she will be a wife, be you a husband, a very husband. When she tells you of her love, upbraid her with her folly; be modishly ungrateful, because she has been unfashionably kind, and use her worse than you would anybody else, because you can't use her so well as she deserves.

PLUME: And are you Silvia, in good earnest?

SILVIA: Earnest! I have gone too far to make it a jest, sir.

PLUME: And do you give her to me in good earnest?

BALANCE: If you please to take her, sir.

PLUME: Why then I have saved my legs and arms, and lost my liberty; secure from wounds, I am prepared for the gout; farewell subsistence, and welcome taxes!—Sir, my liberty, and hopes of being a general, are much dearer to me than your twelve hundred pounds a year.—But to your love, madam, I resign my freedom, and to your beauty and to my ambition: greater in obeying at your feet than commanding at the head of an army.

Enter WORTHY.

WORTHY: I am sorry to hear, Mr Balance, that your daughter is lost.

BALANCE: So am not I, sir, since an honest gentleman has found her.

Enter MELINDA.

MELINDA: Pray, Mr Balance, what's become of my cousin Silvia?

BALANCE: Your cousin Silvia is talking yonder with your cousin Plume.

MELINDA:⎱
⎰ How!
WORTHY:

SILVIA: Do you think it strange, cousin, that a woman should change! But, I hope you'll excuse a change that has proceeded from constancy. I altered my outside, because I was the same within, and only laid by the woman to make sure of my man; that's my history.

MELINDA: Your history is a little romantic, cousin; but since success has crowned your adventures, you will have the world o' your side, and I shall be willing to go with the tide, provided you'll pardon an injury I offered you in the letter to your father.

PLUME: That injury, madam, was done to

me, and the reparation I expect shall be made to my friend: make Mr Worthy happy, and I shall be satisfied.

MELINDA: A good example, sir, will go a long way; when my cousin is pleased to surrender, 'tis probable I sha'n't hold out much longer.

Enter BRAZEN.

BRAZEN: Gentlemen, I am yours.—Madam, I am not yours.

MELINDA: I'm glad on't sir.

BRAZEN: So am I.—You have got a pretty house here, Mr Laconic.

BALANCE: 'Tis time to right all mistakes. My name, sir, is Balance.

BRAZEN: Balance! Sir, I am your most obedient! I know your whole generation. Had not you an uncle that was governor of the Leeward Islands some years ago?

BALANCE: Did you know him?

For once, Brazen lays rightful claim to an acquaintanceship: Balance is astounded.

BRAZEN: Intimately, sir. He played at billiards to a miracle. You had a brother, too, that was captain of a fireship—poor Dick—he had the most engaging way with him—of making punch—and then his cabin was so neat—but his boy Jack was the most comical bastard—ha, ha, ha, ha! a pickled dog, I shall never forget him.

PLUME: Well, Captain, are you fixed in your project yet? are you still for the privateer?

BRAZEN: No, no, I had enough of a privateer just now; I had like to have been picked up by a cruiser under false colours, and a French pickaroon for aught I know.

PLUME: But have you got your recruits, my dear?

BRAZEN: Not a stick, my dear.

PLUME: Probably, I shall furnish you.

Enter ROSE *and* BULLOCK.

ROSE: Captain, Captain, I have got loose once more, and have persuaded my sweet-

heart Cartwheel to go with us; but you must promise not to part with me again.

SILVIA: I find Mrs Rose has not been pleased with her bedfellow.

ROSE: Bedfellow! I don't know whether I had a bedfellow or not.

SILVIA: Don't be in a passion, child; I was as little pleased with your company as you could be with mine.

BULLOCK: Pray, sir, dunna be offended at my sister, she's something underbred; but, if you please, I'll lie with you in her stead.

PLUME: I have promised, madam, to provide for this girl; now will you be pleased to let her wait upon you?or shall I take care of her?

SILVIA: She shall be my charge, sir; you may find it business enough to take care of me.

BULLOCK: Ay, and of me, Captain; for wauns! if ever you lift your hand against me, I'll desart—

PLUME: Captain Brazen shall take care o' that. (*To* BRAZEN) My dear, instead of the twenty thousand pound you talked of, you shall have the twenty brave recruits that I have raised, at the rate they cost me. My commission I lay down, to be taken up by some braver fellow, that has more merit and less good fortune; whilst I endeavour, by the example of this worthy gentleman, to serve my Queen and country at home.

With some regret I quit the active field,
Where glory full reward for life does yield;
But the recruiting trade, with all its train
Of lasting plague, fatigue, and endless
    pain,
I gladly quit, with my fair spouse to stay,
And raise recruits the matrimonial way.

Exeunt.

Kite leads on his ragged band of recruits, with the collier's wife, a solitary camp-follower, bringing up the rear. Plume hands them over to Brazen, who leads them off. The curious words of command used by Brazen were culled for the N.T. production from a military treatise of the period: Soldiers, look lively! Take care of your exercise, bearing your arms well, and keeping due time.

Some Critical Reactions

Irving Wardle in *The Times*: 'Having imported its two best previous productions from Chichester, the National Theatre has at last come forward with a superb production of its own. This version of Farquhar's *The Recruiting Officer* satisfies all the requirements. The play is among the finest Restoration comedies and its revival is long overdue (it was last performed professionally in London 20 years ago): and William Gaskill's direction exemplifies the art of relating a classic to the modern world without distorting the original —the art which gives the National Theatre its cause for existence.

'*The Recruiting Officer* is not a typical Restoration piece. Its provincial setting, its breadth of social characterization, its sexual realism all set the play apart from the charmed circle of fops and wits which dominates the work of Farquhar's contemporaries. In many ways this virile portrait of a Shrewsbury recruiting campaign for Marlborough's army is closer to Jonson than to Congreve—except that Farquhar has no indignation. Brecht, who rewrote the play with an American Civil War setting, gave it a strong element of social protest. But Farquhar, himself a former recruiting officer, saw the corruption and cruelty of the trade, and used it as comic material without advancing any moral conclusions.

'Technically the play's originality springs from the brilliant stroke of fertilizing conventional eighteenth-century comedy with the military theme. The recruiting scenes are dovetailed in a formal love intrigue complete with a jealous father and a female travesty part: the two elements complement one another beautifully—on one side it is natural for the gallants to pursue their girls as if conducting a military campaign, and on the other it is equally natural for them to ensnare their recruits with the tactics of seduction.

'In a programme note Mr Gaskill rightly points out that the play's main point of contact with the modern world is its portrayal of the "systematic deception of the ignorant". Certainly the most concentrated scene in the production is one showing the capture of two reluctant volunteers. The illiterate pair see through the trickery of the sergeant but then fall into the hands of Captain Plume, whose maxim is "those who know the least obey the best", and who conjures up such a glowing vision of the soldiers' life that they capitulate —only to have their ambitions dashed by the point of the sergeant's halberd.

'This scene—which reaches its climax when the two dupes are drawn, mesmerized, towards Plume's outstretched hand—takes one far beyond the regions of comedy. And to that extent it is untypical of the remainder of the production which is, first and foremost, riotously funny.

'From the moment in the first scene when a weather vane drops from the flies and settles on the church with an audible bump, it is plain that the comic spirit has descended on the stage. Rich performances are abundant. Colin Blakely as the wily sergeant, whose villainous past life has ideally prepared him for his present trade, gives a superbly resourceful performance of a military front office man—liberally garnishing his delivery with dropped aitches and genteel vowels. Max Adrian as Justice Balance puts across the character's foxy motives and warmth of heart with copious double-takes and beautifully timed asides; and Maggie Smith, as his outspoken daughter, capitalizes to the full on her possession of free speech in an artificial society. There is also Laurence Olivier as the egregious Captain Brazen—an irrepressible pock-marked vulgarian seen characteristically in a dialogue with a lady during which his gaze travels down from her face until he is addressing his compliments vertically into her bosom.

'Robert Stephens as the protagonist Plume is saddled with an awkward part which undergoes steady moral improvement throughout the play, strait-jacketed to the formal framework of the comedy. (In general, the second half, in which the conventional idiom gains the upper hand, is much less rewarding than the first.) But he handles it with a bravado and directness which almost makes it appear consistent.'

Bamber Gascoigne in the *Observer*: 'The National Theatre production of Farquhar's *The Recruiting Officer* (Old Vic) begins with a touch of magic, and for me the excitement never flagged till the cast had taken its bow.

'When we came in we saw a very drab set, an empty green room with bare walls. I was mentally writing off the designer, René Allio, as a dullard, when the lights went down and his walls began suddenly to crack and swivel. In the blink of an eye the stage was transformed into a little town square, made up of several separate and three-dimensional houses, each one a tiny gem of naturalistic construction. I could have stared happily at them for ages. And I have rarely seen a set which shows off the actors so well. The alleyways between the houses cry out for people to move through them. With simple costumes, also by Allio, and clear lighting by Richard Pilbrow, every scene on this stage acquired an air of sharpened reality, like life on a winter's day with frost and sun.

'This mood is exactly right for Farquhar. His play, written in 1706, adds to the bawdy wit of Restoration comedy a new dash of realism. The plot was based on his own experiences as a recruiting officer in Shrewsbury in 1705. The recruiting scenes widen the play's social scope; and the young Captain Plume, though permanently on the prowl for money and sex, is no foppish court rake. At the end of the play he settles down; in a few years' time a portrait of him as a flabby but respectable gent will take its place on the walls of a country house. Robert Stephens's real success in the part is that he does make Plume just such an ordinary and slightly ungainly young fellow.

'Sergeant Kite, Plume's roguish henchman, is one of Farquhar's most brilliant creations, as rich and thick as a plum pudding. Colin Blakely plays him with huge enjoyment in the accent of a typical sergeant-major, in whose mouth the phrases of the barrack-room are seasoned with an occasional vowel sound from the officers' mess.

'The one truly exotic character is Captain Brazen, a middle-aged flamboyant, a rake long past his time and prime. Olivier gives the old fool a splendidly empty panache. His face is so dissolute that it looks literally on the verge of crumbling. His every gesture is some gross parody of a romantic original, like a cart-horse taking off the winner of the Derby.

'As Silvia, who dresses as a soldier to enlist in Captain Plume's company, Maggie Smith makes a delightful debut with the National Theatre. She is, as usual, frisky, impertinent, bubbling with laughter. In her male disguise she keeps all this just below the surface, but the raising of an eyebrow or the sudden twist of a lip is chink enough for it to come tumbling out.

'In reviving *The Recruiting Officer* and in doing it so well (the director is William Gaskill) the National Theatre has already begun one important part of its purpose—the establishment of a classical British repertoire. And the result, to confound the doubters, is light-years away from the morgue they predicted.'

Harold Hobson in the *Sunday Times*: 'George Farquhar's *The Recruiting Officer*

(Old Vic) is brilliantly written. If one is to have double meanings in a play it is desirable that they should be funny. Farquhar's text about the brutal and lying methods employed in recruiting the soldiers of Good Queen Anne proliferates and burgeons with jokes, suggestions and innuendoes of a sexual and obstetrical kind; it shows that genius will out in this realm as in any other.

'The play is briskly directed by William Gaskill, whose programme notes hint at a certain uneasiness. This is probably due to a subconscious recognition that Farquhar is ahead of his time. Here he defends Chamberlain and the All Souls of the thirties more dazzlingly than they were able to do themselves.

'Maggie Smith's femininely frail redcoat swagger, Laurence Olivier's bleary-eyed impudence as one of the recruiting officers, Max Adrian's fussily complacent Justice of the Peace and Lynn Redgrave's sexily ambitious country bumpkin fairly rock the house with laughter.

'It is inconceivable that *The Recruiting Officer* should not be a popular success. But I have one doubt about the National Theatre. Brecht looms over it. Brecht was a considerable dramatist whose value lay in the tension between his genius and his theories. It will be sad if at the National Theatre we get the theories without the genius.'

Philip Hope-Wallace in the *Guardian*: 'The comedies of George Farquhar deserve a place in the repertory of our National Theatre at the Old Vic and this production of *The Recruiting Officer* (1706) has many happy moments, if no great "follow through" or mounting excitement. The play is weaker in its story line than the more famous "Beaux' Stratagem" of slightly later date, but has the same sort of rustic setting and the charm of Queen Anne's England on its cheek (which is considerable).

'The ruse antedates much in later comedy—"She Stoops to Conquer," for example, or Rossini's "The Philosopher's Stone." The heroine attires herself as a soldier and though she is not required to go to the wars like sweet Polly Oliver, she lands herself with trouble enough in the town of Shrewsbury during a recruiting drive.

'Events culminate in a comic trial which in the playing proved the one dull moment in the present delightful production. I believe that the producer William Gaskill was here trying for some sort of solemn satire of "justice", perhaps in honoured memory of the adaptation of this play which the Berliner Ensemble brought us some years back—in itself rather less good than the Alec Clunes production of 1943, though you'd have a job persuading anyone of that.

'The scenery by René Allio is of the revolving sort and gives us some pleasant brickwork frontages and some easily-set panelled interiors. The clothes and rustic or rakish deportment are excellent. Maggie Smith is not particularly happy in the breeches role as such, but by reason of her own great comic gift pulls off one effect after another with an air of perfect assurance. That is the quality rather lacking, together with a sense of period deportment, in Robert Stephens as the insolent Captain Plume.

'A superb little study of martial inanity (far distant cousin but clearly kin of Saranov in "Arms and the Man") is contributed by Sir Laurence Olivier. This is marvellous from the word go; he makes a subliminal entrance lasting a split second which perfectly forecasts the whole of his performance; a compound of unemphatic swagger and wandering attention, with a vacant eye cocked at nothing in particular. As a performance it quietly outshines the rest. But Colin Blakely manages an amusing portrait of Sergeant Kite (with an "off" accent); Mary Miller, Jeanne Hepple and Lynn Redgrave sketch in ladies of varied stations effectively. This is a good addition to a repertory which is still a little in search of a style, but improves strongly.'

David Pryce-Jones in the *Spectator*: 'Style is what *The Recruiting Officer* needs. It is a lively, highly comic work, and more compact than anything of its time except the best of Congreve. Yet with something so mannered, and in a language both slangy and formalised —almost a dialect—so that it is all the harder to catch the hidden meanings and word-plays, soft or slovenly staging will fix us in our seats with a grin and the stock response "Restoration Comedy" while we wait for the next enlivening episode. Brecht chose to counteract this by re-writing the play, making it into something it is not by assuming that its action arbitrarily suited other circum-stances. Though this was not something one could safely have predicted, the producer at the National Theatre, William Gaskill, has fortunately seen no reason "to put on an English translation of a German adaptation of a perfectly good English play."

'Yet there are concessions. Mr Gaskill has been unable to resist showing Farquhar's "progressiveness", and in the so-called comedy of manners he has discovered a social moral. This is merely to apply contem-porary preoccupations to a work which was conceived quite outside them, something which is anyhow a dull tautology, because we have no alternative, since nobody is reviving 1706. The two countrymen who are pressed into the army were clowns, not victims to Farquhar, and the justices' bench was a riotous satire and not a revelation of military and legal iniquity hand-in-hand.

'Mr Gaskill shows us how simply the the comedy can run by permitting the scenes of conversation to speak for themselves, with characters gliding in and out as for a minuet. This is what we expect from Farquhar and what we ought to get, and if a different, more modern moral is to be drawn, then a different play must be written or else the present work of art will be belittled by being used rather like a poster, which will save us the trouble of thinking out exactly why a work of art and its interpretation are not the same. It would re-quire a producer with an original mind to make something of Farquhar's use of the word "romantic", for instance, which is an innate feature of the play.

'A very successful coup opens the perfor-mance when a frowsty, pre-curtain set re-volves upon itself to break up into a cheerful eighteenth-century market place, allowing great flexibility of entry and space for various drops. This set by René Allio and the hard consistent lighting by Richard Pilbrow are responsible for the good effects of gaiety and colour. The rest is acting. As Captain Brazen, the braggart rake-hell, Laurence Olivier breaks through the production. Like all things so good that one comes to take them for granted, Olivier's skill appears a dependable, but here it is real virtuosity. All decked out with ribbons and tokens, he is a supreme caricature, unrestrained and abun-dant, and so sure of every note that he is never a parody. He has invented several new muscular twitches in his cheeks and contrives to screw his eyes up shortsightedly and provokingly like a bold mouse. It is not just mannerism, however, which fits him for this genre, but a way of rounding his sentences, and finishing his sentences with correct em-phasis, as if he were playing a harpsichord. This modulation is exactly the style required to enhance the comedy.

'Max Adrian has it too. The part of Justice Balance is rather cruder and not just less flamboyant, but Max Adrian brings out an authenticity and a fullness which are almost pedantic and which make a far sharper com-ment than anything the production can con-trive. This is all one needs to know about justices of the peace, and none of the mar-shalling of prisoners in the courtroom (where it says "mob" in the text, by the way) will add to it.

'Robert Stephens is the decent Captain Plume who gives up his military career for the girl he loves. All men are honest under-neath, seems to be the maxim, but with most of them you have to go a long way down. Robert Stephens shows an unusual turn for forthright comedy; he can provoke the hec-toring laugh which underlies so much of English humour. One measure of his increas-ing stature these days is that he looks physi-

143

cally bigger with each new part. Only Maggie Smith leaves it to her lines to try their luck without her help. Perhaps she is tired, for her flair was missing and she relies for her chief effect on a stock device of hers, to slur the ends of the sentences glissando, while raising her voice as if everything were the one big throw-away it becomes.'

Roger Gellert in the *New Statesman*: 'The National Theatre's fourth show and second new production, *The Recruiting Officer*, is a sort of 1706 Army Game based on Farquhar's personal observations as just such an officer in just such a recruiting drive in simple-minded Shrewsbury. The methods, as demonstrated by Sergeant Kite in the play, were brutally direct: get your victim drunk, slip a queen's shilling into his pocket, confront him with it when he wakes. But, for all that William Gaskill can do to bring out the cruel implications, Farquhar soon loses sight of any satirical aim he may have had and modulates into curious though very funny transvestite farce, when Captain Plume's inamorata Silvia (Maggie Smith) dons a moustache, breeches and manly scarlet but finds herself warmly invited to share a bed by her duped Plume (Robert Stephens) and less ambiguously chased by his monstrous recruiting rival Captain Brazen (Laurence Olivier). Oscar Wilde, it seems, would have been happy in Queen Anne's army, where "an officer and his man are like husband and wife: always fighting or kissing." Brazen in particular is randy for anything in or out of breeches; and the picture of Olivier (a clothes-horse of ludicrous seedy panache under a billow of white plumage and black curls flopping in baby-blue bows on his shoulders) impartially greeting Plume and his fellow-warriors with a cry of "my dear!" and a hearty buss, or hovering in a cod-like trance over some ripe young country cleavage is what one inevitably treasures most.

'Less fantastically, Stephens's Plume is magnificent. This lean man with the look, snarl and yelp of a hungry dog has never been a graceful actor, but besides the expected houndish bite he has the gift to be astonishingly and movingly simple, and the delicacy of feeling in his overtures to the "fair youth", is quite breathtaking. Maggie Smith, as Silvia, is more plainly waggish, her odd nasal chortle as apt for the pleasing perversions of army life as for the spleen of a night of ill-feigned passion with a resentful country girl (Lynn Redgrave). I found Colin Blakely's rendering of the egregious Kite a disappointment, for he has overlaid his fine native Ulster with an unconvincing veneer of conventional bullying refinement. There are, too, some flabbily unfunny scenes and a typically awful straight romantic sub-plot. But in its chaotic way *The Recruiting Officer* is certainly a riot, with a ravishing set of twiddlable Shrewsbury houses (bricked-in windows and all) by René Allio.'